Web Services

Building Blocks for Distributed Systems

D1451481

ISBN 013066256-9

90000

9 780130 662569

Web Services

Building Blocks for Distributed Systems

Graham Glass

PRENTICE HALL PTR
UPPER SADDLE RIVER, NJ 07458
WWW.PHPTR.COM

Editorial/production supervision: *Mary Sudul*
Composition: *FASTpages*
Acqusition Editor: *Paul Petralia*
Editorial Assistant: *Richard Winkler*
Marketing Manager: *Debby vanDijk*
Manufacturing Manager: *Alexis R. Heydt*
Cover Design: *Design Source*
Cover Design Director: *Jerry Votta*
Series Design: *Gail Cocker-Bogusz*

© 2002 Prentice Hall PTR
Prentice-Hall, Inc.
Upper Saddle River, NJ 07458

The publisher offers discounts on this book when ordered in bulk quantities.
For more information, contact
Corporate Sales Department,
Prentice Hall PTR
One Lake Street
Upper Saddle River, NJ 07458
Phone: 800-382-3419; FAX: 201-236-714
E-mail (Internet): corpsales@prenhall.com

Printed in the United States of America

10 9 8 7 6 5 4 3 2 1

ISBN 0-13-066256-9

Pearson Education LTD.
Pearson Education Australia PTY, Limited
Pearson Education Singapore, Pte. Ltd
Pearson Education North Asia Ltd
Pearson Education Canada, Ltd.
Pearson Educación de Mexico, S.A. de C.V.
Pearson Education — Japan
Pearson Education Malaysia, Pte. Ltd
Pearson Education, Upper Saddle River, New Jersey

This book is dedicated to my parents, whose continued love and support helps me to weather the storms.

And to my three gorgeous kitties.

Contents

Preface

About the Author

Graham Glass is the chief architect and founder of The Mind Electric, a company that builds and licenses forward thinking distributed computing infrastructure. He became interested in the workings of the mind at the age of 4, and decided early in his career that large-scale distributed computing was the best place to make progress in that area.

He believes that the evolution of the Internet will mirror that of a biological mind, and that architectures for helping people and businesses to network effectively will provide insight into those that wire together the human brain.

Prior to founding The Mind Electric, Graham was the CTO and co-founder of ObjectSpace, a Dallas-based company specializing in distributed computing. At ObjectSpace, he was the architect and lead developer of the Voyager product line, the JGL Java collections library, and the cross-platform C++ toolkits. Graham received an Ernst and Young Entrepreneur of the Year award in 1996, as well as several industry awards for Voyager and JGL.

Graham was also the founder of ObjectLesson, a company that provided training in leading-edge technologies. He authored two books for Prentice Hall on the subjects of UNIX and STL, and is a popular public speaker known for his enthusiasm and clear explanations of emerging technologies.

He earned his Bachelor of Science in Mathematics and Computer Science from the University of Southampton, his Master of Science in Computer Science from the University of Texas at Dallas, and his British "O" and "A" levels from Haberdashers' Aske's School in Elstree. Before moving into Industry, he taught UNIX, C, C++, Smalltalk and Programming Languages as a senior lecturer at UTD.

Graham's passion is creating the kind of world that currently only exists in science fiction books. In his spare time, he works.

Acknowledgments

I'd like to thank Paul Petralia at Prentice Hall for his help and encouragement in bringing this book from concept to fruition. In addition, I'd like to thank Tony Hong, Paul Kulchenko, and the rest of the enthusiasts on the SOAPBuilders interest group for working so hard to make SOAP interoperable.

Contact Information

You can contact Graham at graham@themindelectric.com, and visit his company's web site at http://www.themindelectric.com.

Feedback

We'd love to hear your comments and suggestions. Please send any feedback you have to graham@themindelectric.com. We'll be sure to acknowledge good ideas in subsequent editions of this book.

Introduction

It seems like only yesterday that I was sitting behind a computer terminal writing my first book for Prentice Hall. The book, titled *UNIX for Programmers and Users*, was released in 1993 and is still going strong. During that period, I was getting involved in distributed computing for the first time, and wrote simple C programs that used sockets to send data back and forth on a network. My first experience of network programming was so exciting and powerful that I decided to dedicate the last chapter of my UNIX book to a concept called *The Grid*, a term that I gave to a pervasive global network linking all computers, from mainframes to cell phones. Here is one of my favorite quotes from the book:

"Home appliances, cars, industrial robots and other machines will all be part of the Grid. In other words, everything will talk to everything. Resources and their interconnectivity will be greater than ever before. The theme of the 21st century will be collaboration."

Because the chapter was a bit off topic, and the Internet was virtually unknown in 1993, Prentice Hall removed it from the second edition of the book. Funnily enough, the quote is now perfect for this introduction to my new book on web services—a technology that is sweeping the computing industry and will forever change the way we think about distributed systems.

It gives me great pleasure to continue what I started to write all those years ago, and to provide you with a good understanding of the next logical step in the evolution of distributed computing.

Sincerely,

Graham Glass
August 2001

How to Use This Book

The chapters progress naturally from web services basics to futuristic advanced stuff.

Chapter 1 provides an introduction to web services and describes the main concepts and terms. It's a great way to get acquainted with the topic, and can be used as a stand-alone primer before going to a web services presentation or conference.

To get hands-on experience, proceed to Chapter 2 which guides you through the process of building and invoking a simple web service. This chapter also shows you how to access and manage web services from a web browser, as well as perform common tasks such as aggregation.

Once you've seen how easy it is to create a web service, you'll want to read Chapters 3 through 6, which cover more advanced topics such as Web Services Description Language (WSDL), security and Universal Description, Discovery, and Integration (UDDI). Each of these topics is explained with the help of hands-on examples.

Chapters 7 through 9 show how the popular .NET and Java 2 Enterprise Edition (J2EE) platforms support web services, and how you can build systems that incorporate web services written using both of these technologies.

The final chapter offers a glimpse of where web services is going, with a discussion of the trend toward decentralization and peer-to-peer computing.

Web Services

Web services is one of the most exciting new developments in the field of computer science, and also one of the most misunderstood. Some people describe it as a technology designed strictly for publishing software services to the Internet, whereas others think of it as a general-purpose architecture that will trigger a fundamental shift in the way that all distributed systems are created. As you'll see shortly, I definitely believe the latter.

This chapter provides an introduction to web services that shows it is not a fad but a natural and logical evolution of distributed computing. It covers all of the important terms such as SOAP, WSDL, and UDDI, as well as touching upon common questions related to performance and reliability.

The chapter ends with a fun story that strongly influenced my interest in distributed computing and offers a glimpse of where web services might lead.

GLUE, my company's web services platform, is used for the first few chapters of this book because it is easy to learn, installs without hassle, and is free for most commercial uses. Later in the book I introduce some examples that use Microsoft .NET and J2EE, and show how these systems can interoperate using SOAP.

If you want to follow along with the examples, now is a good time to read the appendix section titled "Installing GLUE and the Examples."

What is a Web Service?

A *software service* is something that accepts digital requests and returns digital responses. Using this definition, a C function, a Java object, and a Structure Query Language (SQL)-stored procedure are all examples of software services; a computer application can be thought of as a well-orchestrated set of services.

Until now, a specific software service could only be used within a particular language or platform, and was often not accessible across a network. *Web services* are a new breed of software component that is language, platform, and location independent. They are Extensible Markup Language (XML)-based building blocks for the next generation of applications whose parts can reside in a single machine or span the globe.

The term *web service* is unfortunately a bit misleading, because many people think that it means a service specialized for use across the World Wide Web. This leads to opinions like "web services will fail because there won't be enough demand for subscriptions to Internet software services." In fact, the term is an abbrevation for *Web of Services*, meaning that distributed applications will be assembled from a web of software services in the same way that web sites are assembled from a web of HTML pages. If there's one thing that I hope to convince you of, it's that a majority of distributed applications will be built out of web services, regardless of whether they are deployed to a single machine, a corporate intranet, or the Internet (see Figure 1.1).

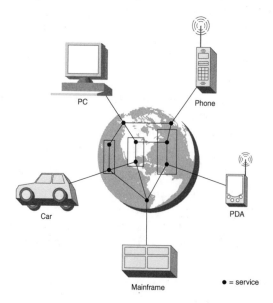

FIGURE 1.1

In the future, distributed systems will be webs of services

There is much debate as to whether web services are an evolution or a revolution. My view on this issue was expressed in the title of a column I wrote for IBM developerWorks. The column was called "The Web Services (R)evolution" because I think that web services are both an evolution of distributed computing and the launch point for a revolution in the way we think about building large-scale systems. To fully appreciate the impact of web services, it's useful to study their ancestry.

Let's take a look at the evolution of software services.

The Evolution of Software Services

In the early days, computer programs were written in assembly language and executed in a single memory space. The software services in this case were subroutines written in assembly language, and they communicated digitally via machine registers. Programs written in this way were not portable, and hard to write and maintain.

Soon after assembly language came procedural languages like FORTRAN and COBOL, which provided a layer of abstraction so that programs could be written more easily and run on different machines. The software services in this case were functions that were orchestrated by control structures, and, like assembly subroutines, they all executed in a single memory space (see Figure 1.2).

Network computing followed soon after, allowing systems to exchange information in real-time instead of having to transfer data using magnetic tapes. The UNIX operating system had built-in support for the Transmission Control Protocol/Internet Protocol (TCP/IP) network protocol, and C became the most popular language for writing network applications. A technique called

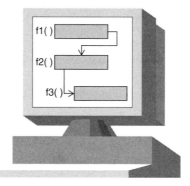

FIGURE 1.2
Functions communicating within a single memory space

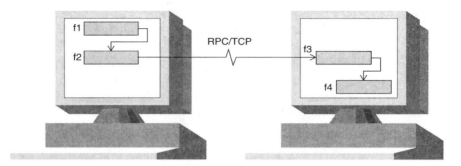

FIGURE 1.3
Functions communicating between memory spaces using RPC

Remote Procedure Call (RPC) was invented to allow functions written in C, FORTRAN or any other procedural language to invoke each other across a network, allowing software services to break free from the confines of individual machines and collaborate on a large scale. A protocol called eXternal Data Representation (XDR) allowed complex data structures to be sent between functions regardless of platform or language (see Figure 1.3).

After procedural languages came functional languages like LISP and object-oriented languages like C++, which provided still higher levels of abstraction and allowed developers to create software objects that resembled their real-world counterparts. And as you've probably guessed, an object is yet another example of a software service, only this time it happens to encapsulate its behavior and support polymorphism. New distributed computing protocols were designed to allow objects to communicate in a more natural fashion than RPC, and the most successful were CORBA (Common Object Request Broker Architecture) and DCOM (Distributed Common Object Model). A consortium of large companies supported CORBA, including IBM, Oracle and Sun, whereas DCOM came from a single vendor, namely Microsoft. Most early deployments of these technologies were in homogenous, closed environments (see Figure 1.4).

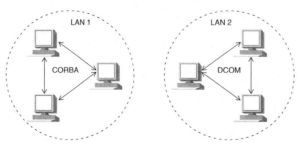

FIGURE 1.4
Two LANs, one using CORBA and one using DCOM

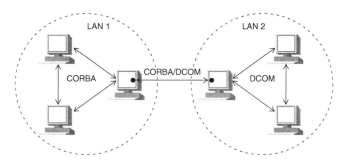

FIGURE 1.5
Two LANs, connected using a CORBA/DCOM bridge

Regardless of their relative technical merits, the most annoying thing for developers was that CORBA and DCOM were incompatible, and it was hard work to get them to communicate with each other. If you wanted to link systems that used different protocols, you would typically install protocol converters on each gateway (see Figure 1.5).

Then the Internet burst onto the scene. Thanks to the inventions of Tim Berners-Lee, anyone could use a browser to surf and enjoy the vast amount of information stored on millions of computers around the world. Traditional geographic barriers started to fall, and consumers were able to purchase from any company that had a web site. The Internet is based on a single, simple set of open standards. HyperText Transport Protocol (HTTP), the transport protocol for sharing data between machines, is quick to implement and rides on top of the ubiquitous lower-level TCP/IP protocol. And HyperText Markup Language (HTML), the format for representing data in a browser-friendly way, can be understood by a teenager in a few hours. Ease of use certainly helped the adoption of the Internet (see Figure 1.6).

The Internet opened a lot of people's eyes to the power of distributed computing, and businesses started investing more time into harnessing the power of networking. But although HTTP and HTML made it easier for consumers to access remote web pages, they didn't simplify the integration of business systems. *What was missing was a way to share data and software services across the Internet.*

The sharing of data was addressed by XML, a more sophisticated and general-purpose version of HTML that allows any kind of data to be represented in a simple and portable way. By surrounding data with tags that indicate its meaning, XML documents are self-describing and can be easily manipulated and transformed (see Figure 1.7).

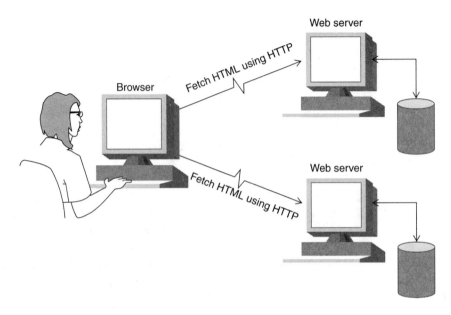

FIGURE 1.6
HTML and HTTP make it easy for people to share content across the Internet

```
<invoice id = '13522'>
    <item>  football  <\item>
    <amount>  39.95  <\amount>
<\invoice>
```

FIGURE 1.7
A simple XML document

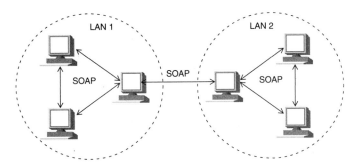

FIGURE 1.8
SOAP is a universal protocol for connecting everything

The sharing of services, which is basically what this book is all about, is being tackled by a new set of standards called SOAP[1] (Service-Oriented Architecture Protocol), WSDL (Web Services Description Language) and UDDI (Universal Description, Discovery, and Integration). Built on top of HTTP and XML, these standards allow software services to be published, located and invoked in a way that is language, platform and location independent. Software building blocks created and deployed using this technology are called *web services* (see Figure 1.8).

Web services are important because they greatly simplify the creation and integration of large-scale distributed systems. In the same way that HTML catalyzed a vast web of human-accessible content, SOAP, WSDL, and UDDI will enable a web of machine-accessible services. Let's take a closer look at these three key technologies.

SOAP

SOAP is the new standard for network communication between software services. It is a general-purpose technology for sending messages between endpoints, and may be used for RPC or straightforward document transfer. SOAP messages are represented using XML and can be sent over any transport layer. HTTP is the most common transport layer, with implementations also available for Simple Mail Transport Protocol (SMTP), Java Messaging Service (JMS), and IBM MQSeries (see Figure 1.9).

---

1. SOAP officially stands for Simple Object Access Protocol, but since SOAP is neither simple nor object-oriented, the term has been informally redefined.

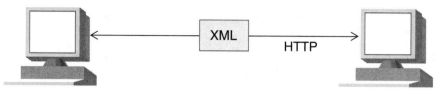

FIGURE 1.9
SOAP messages are XML documents, usually sent over HTTP

The easiest way to publish a software component as a web service is to use a
SOAP container which accepts incoming requests and dispatches them to
published components, automatically translating between SOAP and the
component's native language interface. SOAP containers are available for
most programming languages, including Java, C++, Perl, and C# (see Figure
1.10).

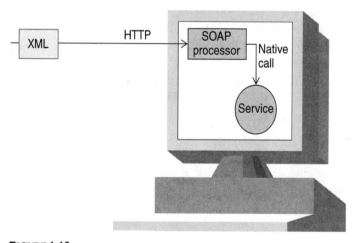

FIGURE 1.10
A SOAP container converts XML messages into native calls

Once a component has been published as a web service, any SOAP-enabled
client that knows the network address of the service and the messages that it
understands can send a SOAP request and get back a SOAP response. To get
the address and message information, SOAP clients read a WSDL file that
describes the web service. Fortunately, most SOAP containers will automatically generate WSDL for the web services that they host, so developers don't
have to write WSDL manually unless they really want to. Once the WSDL
file is read, the client can start sending SOAP messages to the web service
(see Figure 1.11).

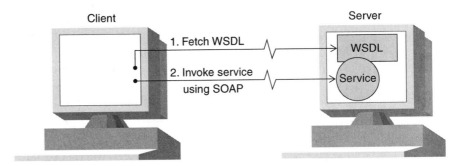

FIGURE 1.11
A client needs WSDL before invoking the service

Publishing a Web Service

Before delving into the details of the SOAP protocol, I'll show you how easy it is to create and invoke a web service using a modern language like Java. The main thing to note is that no knowledge of SOAP or WSDL is necessary to immediately become a productive web services developer.

The following example shows the steps that are necessary to publish an object as a web service and then invoke it from a SOAP client. Although most examples in this book are written in Java, it is important to note that SOAP is language neutral and can support any combination of languages on the client and server. Some examples of Java programs talking to C# programs using SOAP are presented in the .NET chapter.

The object in this example is a simple stock trading service that defines a single method for buying stock. The buy() method returns the cost of purchasing a specified quantity of a particular stock. Here is the source code for the ITrader interface.

wsbook\src\book\soap\ITrader.java

```
package book.soap;

/**
 * An interface for buying stock.
 */
public interface ITrader
    {
    /**
     * Purchase the specified stock.
```

```
 * @param quantity The number of shares to purchase.
 * @param symbol The ticker symbol of the company.
 * @throws TradeException If the symbol is not recognized.
 * @return The cost of the purchase.
 */
float buy( int quantity, String symbol ) throws TradeException;
}
```

The Trader class is a simple implementation of ITrader that uses hard-coded stock prices and throws an exception if it doesn't recognize a particular ticker symbol.

wsbook\src\book\soap\Trader.java

```java
package book.soap;

/**
 * Simple implementation of ITrader.
 */
public class Trader implements ITrader
  {
  public float buy( int quantity, String symbol )
    throws TradeException
    {
    if( symbol.equals( "IBM" ) )
      return 117.4F * quantity;
    else if( symbol.equals( "MSFT" ) )
      return 68.1F * quantity;
    else
      throw new TradeException( "symbol " + symbol + " not
recognized" );
    }
  }
```

Notice that neither the interface nor the source code for the trader service contains any code related to SOAP or web services. Most SOAP containers are able to publish unmodified software components, which is good because domain objects should not be coupled to details of distributed computing.

Each SOAP container has different Application Programming Interfaces (APIs) for starting up an in-process HTTP server and for publishing objects as web services. Here is the way that you would start an HTTP server on http://localhost:8003/soap and export an instance of Trader using GLUE, the web services platform included with this book. GLUE is described in more detail in the next chapter.

wsbook\src\book\soap\TraderServer.java

```java
package book.soap;

import electric.registry.Registry;
import electric.server.http.HTTP;

public class TraderServer
  {
  public static void main( String[] args )
    throws Exception
    {
    // start a web server on port 8003, accept messages via /soap
    HTTP.startup( "http://localhost:8003/soap" );

    // publish an instance of Trader
    Registry.publish( "trader", new Trader() );
    }
  }
```

Binding to a Web Service

Once an object is published as a web service, a SOAP client can bind to it
and invoke it. For example, here's what a SOAP client written using GLUE
looks like. Fortunately, from a Java developer's viewpoint, a web service can
be invoked as if it were a local object, with all the details of SOAP and WSDL
hidden by the underlying infrastructure. Microsoft .NET provides a similar
mechanism for C# and Visual Basic developers.

wsbook\src\book\soap\TraderClient.java

```java
package book.soap;

import electric.registry.Registry;

public class TraderClient
  {
  public static void main( String[] args ) throws Exception
    {
    // the URL of the web service WSDL file
    String url = "http://localhost:8003/soap/trader.wsdl";

    // read the WSDL file and bind to its associated web service

    ITrader trader = (ITrader) Registry.bind( url, ITrader.class );

    // invoke the web service as if it was a local object
    float ibmCost = trader.buy( 54, "IBM" );
    System.out.println( "IBM cost is " + ibmCost );
```

```
    float tmeCost = trader.buy( 32, "TME" );
    System.out.println( "TME cost is " + tmeCost );
    }
}
```

The binding process returns a proxy that implements a Java interface whose methods mirror those of the remote service. A message sent to the proxy is automatically converted into a SOAP request, delivered across the network, and the SOAP response is converted back into a regular Java result.

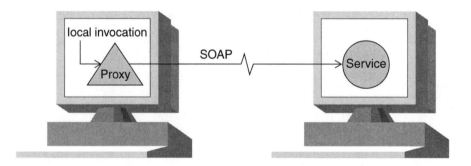

FIGURE 1.12
A client proxy hides the communication details from the application

When the `TraderClient` is executed, SOAP messages fly back and forth between the client and server, translated automatically between XML and native calls by the SOAP container. The first method succeeds and returns a value, whereas the second method throws an exception because the symbol `TME` is not recognized.

Here is the server output:

```
> java book.soap.TraderServer
GLUE 1.2 (c) 2001 The Mind Electric
startup server on http://199.174.20.117:8003/soap
```

Here is the client output:

```
> java book.soap.TraderClient
IBM cost is 6339.6
Exception in thread "main" book.soap.TradeException: symbol TME not
recognized

> _
```

This example hopefully has convinced you that web services programs can be written without any detailed knowledge of SOAP or WSDL. Now let's examine the SOAP messages in detail.

Anatomy of a SOAP Request

Here's what the SOAP request looks like when the example client sends a buy() message, with the method and arguments highlighted for clarity.

```
POST /soap/trader HTTP/1.1
Host: 199.174.18.220:8004
Content-Type: text/xml
User-Agent: GLUE/1.0
Connection: Keep-Alive
SOAPAction: "buy"
Content-Length: 525

<?xml version='1.0' encoding='UTF-8'?>
<soap:Envelope
  xmlns:soap='http://schemas.xmlsoap.org/soap/envelope/'
  xmlns:xsi='http://www.w3.org/2001/XMLSchema-instance'
  xmlns:xsd='http://www.w3.org/2001/XMLSchema'
  xmlns:soapenc='http://schemas.xmlsoap.org/soap/encoding/'
  soap:encodingStyle='http://schemas.xmlsoap.org/soap/encoding/'>
  <soap:Body>
    <n:buy xmlns:n='http://tempuri.org/book.soap.Trader'>
      <quantity xsi:type='xsd:int'>54</quantity>
      <symbol xsi:type='xsd:string'>IBM</symbol>
    </n:buy>
  </soap:Body>
</soap:Envelope>
```

Even without an explanation of the SOAP format, you can probably figure out what most of it means. Contrast this with the CORBA and DCOM protocols, which are binary, not self-describing, and tough to trace. I know this firsthand, having written a CORBA ORB in a previous lifetime.

The first part of the SOAP request is a standard HTTP header that indicates that the request is an HTTP POST operation whose Universal Resource Identifier (URI) is /soap/trader. The Content-Type field shows that the HTTP payload is XML, and the SOAPAction field tells the remote host that the content is a SOAP message. SOAPAction is often set to the name of the method to invoke so that the host web server or firewall can perform some high-level message filtering.

The second part of the SOAP request is an XML document that consists of three main portions:

Envelope   The envelope defines the various XML namespaces that are used by the rest of the SOAP message, and typically include xmlns:soap (SOAP envelope namespace), xmlns:xsi (XML Schema for instances), xmlns:xsd (XML Schema for data types) and xmlns:soapenc (SOAP encoding namespace). More information about these namespaces is presented later in this book.

Header   The header is an optional element for carrying auxiliary information for authentication, transactions, routing, and payments. Any element in a SOAP processing chain can add or delete items from the header; elements can also choose to ignore items if they are unknown. If a header is present, it must be the first child of the envelope. Because our example is simple and does not invoke routers, the header is absent.

Body   The body is the main payload of the message. When SOAP is used to perform an RPC call, the body contains a single element that contains the method name and arguments. The namespace of the method name is specified by the web service, and in this case is equal to http://tempuri.org/ followed by the type of the target web service. The type of each argument can be optionally supplied using the xsi:type attribute; in this example, the first argument is flagged as an xsd:int, and the second argument as an xsd:string. If a header is present, the body must be its immediate sibling; otherwise it must be the first child of the envelope.

A SOAP request is typically accepted by a servlet, CGI or standalone daemon running on the remote web server. In this example, the GLUE SOAP container started a servlet running on localhost:8003/soap. When the servlet gets a request, it checks that the request has a SOAPAction field, and if it does, forwards it to the SOAP container. The container uses the POST URI to look up the target web service, parses the XML payload, and then invokes the method on the component.

Anatomy of a SOAP Response

The result of the invocation is translated by the SOAP container into a SOAP response and returned back to the sender within the HTTP reply. Here's the SOAP response from the `buy()` message sent to the `Trader` service, with the result name and value highlighted for clarity.

```
HTTP/1.1 200 OK
Date: Sat, 19 May 2001 06:58:38 GMT
Content-Type: text/xml
Server: GLUE/1.0
Content-Length: 489

<?xml version='1.0' encoding='UTF-8'?>
<soap:Envelope
  xmlns:soap='http://schemas.xmlsoap.org/soap/envelope/'
  xmlns:xsi='http://www.w3.org/2001/XMLSchema-instance'
  xmlns:xsd='http://www.w3.org/2001/XMLSchema'
  xmlns:soapenc='http://schemas.xmlsoap.org/soap/encoding/'
  soap:encodingStyle='http://schemas.xmlsoap.org/soap/encoding/'>
  <soap:Body>
    <n:buyResponse xmlns:n='http://tempuri.org/book.soap.Trader'>
      <Result xsi:type='xsd:float'>6339.6</Result>
    </n:buyResponse>
  </soap:Body>
</soap:Envelope>
```

The XML document is structured just like the request except that the body contains the encoded method result. By convention, the name of the result is equal to the name of the method followed by "Response", and the namespace of the result is the same as the namespace of the original method.

SOAP Exceptions

If an exception occurs at any time during the processing of a message, a SOAP fault is generated and encoded in a manner similar to a regular SOAP response. Here is the SOAP response that is returned when our example client attempts to buy stock for a ticker symbol that is not recognized.

```
HTTP/1.1 500 Internal Server Error
Content-Type: text/xml
Content-Length: 244

<soap:Fault>
  <faultcode>soap:Server</faultcode>
  <faultstring>symbol TME not recognized</faultstring>
  <detail>
    <stacktrace>
      book.soap.TradeException: symbol TME not recognized
        at book.soap.Trader.buy(Trader.java:16)
        at java.lang.reflect.Method.invoke(Native Method)
    </stacktrace>
  </detail>
</soap:Fault>
```

The standard HTTP reply header indicates an exception by using status code 500. The XML payload contains an envelope and body just like a regular response, except that the content of the body is a `soap:Fault` structure whose fields are defined as follows:

faultcode	A code that indicates the type of the fault. The valid values are `soap:Client` (incorrectly formed message), `soap:Server` (delivery problem), `soap:VersionMismatch` (invalid namespace for `Envelope` element) and `soap:MustUnderstand` (error processing header content).
faultstring	A human readable description of the fault.
faultactor	An optional field that indicates the URL of the source of the fault.
detail	An application-specific XML document that contains detailed information about the fault.

Some SOAP implementations add an additional element to encode information about remote exceptions such as their type, data, and stack trace so that they can be rethrown automatically on the client.

Performance

Now that you've seen how SOAP messages are passed back and forth using HTTP and XML, it is time to contemplate performance issues.

CORBA and DCOM use binary encoding for arguments and return values. In addition, they assume that both the sender and the receiver have full knowledge of the message context and do not encode any meta-information such as the names or types of the arguments. This approach results in good performance, but makes it hard for intermediaries to process messages. And since each system uses a different binary encoding, it's hard to build systems that interoperate.

Because SOAP uses XML to encode messages, it's very easy to process messages at every step of the invocation process. In addition, the ease of debugging SOAP messages is leading to a quick convergence of the various SOAP implementations, which is important because large-scale interoperability is what SOAP is all about.

On the surface, it seems that an XML-based scheme would be intrinsically slower than that of a binary-based model, but it's not as straightforward as that.

First, when SOAP is used for sending messages across the Internet, the time to encode/decode the messages at each endpoint is tiny compared with the time to transfer bytes between endpoints, so using XML in this case is not significant.

Second, when SOAP is used to send messages between endpoints in a closed environment, such as between departments within the same company, it's likely that the endpoints will be running the same implementation of SOAP. In this case, there are opportunities for optimizations that are unique to that particular implementation. For example, a SOAP client could add an HTTP header tag to a SOAP request that indicates that it supports a particular optimization. If the SOAP server also supports that optimization, it could return an HTTP header tag in the first SOAP response that tells the client that it's okay to use that optimization in subsequent communications. At that point, both the client and the server could start using the optimization.

The fastest SOAP implementations typically get at least 500 messages/second on a 600MHz desktop PC when the client and the server are in different programs in the same machine, and around 300 messages/second on a fast local area network (LAN).

Other SOAP Features

The example in this section was very simple and demonstrated only a subset of SOAP functionality. Additional features, many of which are covered later in this book, include:

- Arrays, objects, and other complex data structures may be sent across the network in a platform and language neutral way.
- SOAP headers support security, transactions, and routing.
- Custom encoding types may be defined.
- SOAP supports request-response, one-way, solicit-response, and notification operations.

Now that you've seen what SOAP messaging looks like, it's time to look at WSDL.

WSDL

WSDL is the XML equivalent of a resume—it describes what a web service can do, where it resides, and how to invoke it. If you're familiar with CORBA or COM, think of WSDL as the web services equivalent of Interface Definition Language (IDL) and type libraries.

One of the main ideas behind web services is that applications of the future will be assembled from a collection of network-enabled services. As long as two equivalent services are able to advertise themselves to the network in a standard and neutral way, an application could theoretically choose between alternative competing services based on criteria such as price or performance. In addition, some services could be copied between machines, enabling an application to improve its performance by dynamically installing services into its local storage.

If you think about it, this is similar to how the human labor market works. Job sites and recruiting companies provide a matchmaking service between workers and employees, utilizing resumes and job descriptions to facilitate the matching process. If a good match is found, the interested parties attempt to negotiate acceptable terms. If an agreement is reached, the worker either moves to the employer's location or takes advantage of the Internet and telecommutes instead.

To get a sneek peek at a WSDL file, run the `TraderServer` program from the previous section, then enter http://localhost:8003/soap/trader.wsdl into your web browser. The WSDL for the trader web service is displayed, and should look like Figure 1.13.

The meaning of the various fields in a WSDL file are described in the WSDL chapter, together with information about how to use WSDL to automatically generated client-side bindings for a web service.

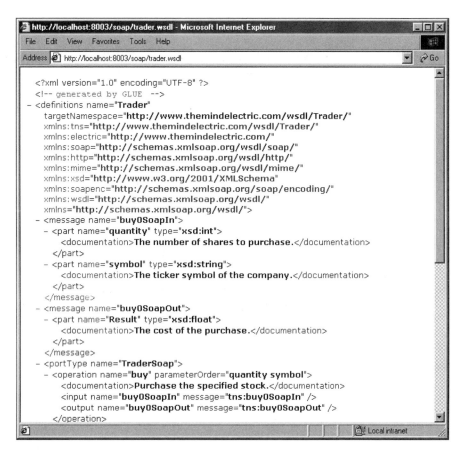

FIGURE 1.13
The trader web service WSDL

Now that we have a way to describe the characteristics of a web service, we need a way to publish the WSDL so that other SOAP clients can find the service and bind to it. Let's take a look at UDDI, the web services matchmaker.

UDDI

UDDI is a new standard that allows information about businesses and services to be electronically published and queried. Published information is stored into one or more UDDI registries, which can be accessed through a web browser or via SOAP. Here's an example of how UDDI will be used in the future.

Let's say that Acme Credit makes a living by performing credit checks. In the past, a customer would fax Acme information about the subject of the credit check, and would receive a faxed credit report. Acme maintains a staff of data entry clerks who enter the contents of a fax into the Acme computer system, print the credit report, and then fax it to the customer. While this is certainly workable, it is expensive to scale and not very fast. To improve the system and make their credit checking system directly available to other computer systems, Acme decides to adopt web services.

In the first phase of adoption, Acme creates a web service that exposes a set of credit check operations to any SOAP client. The web service itself is a thin wrapper that accepts incoming SOAP requests, invokes them on the Acme credit system, then returns the result as a SOAP response. Acme also generates a WSDL file that describes the web service so that other SOAP clients can invoke it. Acme makes the WSDL available to its current customers, who love it because their computer systems can now quickly perform credit checks via SOAP across the Internet without having to involve humans and fax machines (see Figure 1.14).

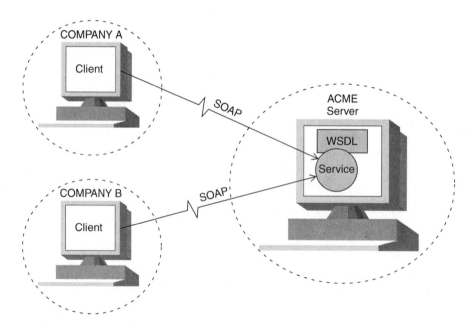

FIGURE 1.14
Clients can invoke the Acme credit service across the Internet

In the second phase of adoption, Acme decides to make its credit service available to a broader audience. It goes to one of the popular UDDI sites, obtains a user/password, and enters general information about Acme such as its name, address, contact information, and category. Acme also registers its credit check web service, including its endpoint address and a reference to its WSDL. At this point, other companies can locate Acme through a browser, learn about its services, and create SOAP clients that invoke its credit check operations. In addition, SOAP clients can search the UDDI registry using SOAP messages and locate the Acme credit service at run time. As a result of making its credit check system available as a web service, Acme sees its customer base grow rapidly and enters a new phase of growth (see Figure 1.15).

In the third phase of adoption, the Acme credit service becomes so popular that its WSDL interface specification is adopted by the credit industry as a standard, and other companies start to publish alternative competing implementations of the interface to UDDI. Although this means more competition for Acme, it also strengthens its position as a thought leader.

The three public UDDI registries, hosted by IBM, Microsoft, and HP, synchronize contents regularly so that information entered into one is quickly

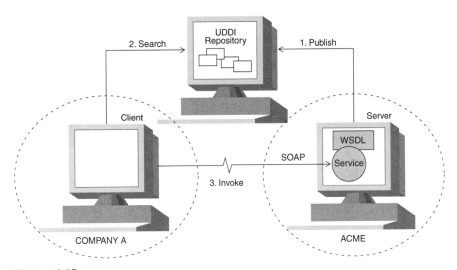

FIGURE 1.15
UDDI acts as a matchmaker for providers and consumers of web services

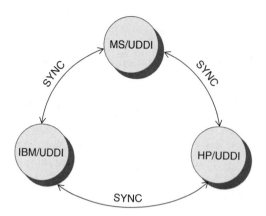

FIGURE 1.16
Public UDDI operators synchronize their contents regularly

replicated to the others. To assist developers in understanding UDDI, each company also hosts a test registry that is intended for educational purposes (see Figure 1.16).

Many companies are contemplating establishing their own private UDDI registries for cataloging their internal web services. Indeed, several industry pundits believe that UDDI will be adopted in intranet environments quicker than on the Internet.

The UDDI section of this book contains an in-depth description of UDDI, as well as several examples.

Web Services Adoption

Even though SOAP, WSDL, and UDDI are young standards, I think they're pretty much guaranteed to be at the heart of the next generation of distributed systems. Here's why:

Interoperability	Any web service can interact with any other web service. Thanks to SOAP, the agonies of converting between CORBA, DCOM, and other protocols are over. And because web services can be written in any programming language, developers do not need to change environments in order to produce or consume web services.

Ubiquity	Web services communicate using HTTP and XML. Any device that supports these standards can host and access web services. Pretty soon, they will be present in phones, cars, and even soda machines. Soda supplies getting low? No problem, the wireless-networked soda machine will contact the local supplier's web service and order more.
Low Barrier to Entry	The concepts behind web services are easy to understand and toolkits are freely available from many vendors. In addition, some toolkits allow pre-existing components to be published instantly as web services, thus accelerating the early adoption of this technology.
Industry Support	All of the major vendors are supporting SOAP and the surrounding web services standards. For example, the Microsoft .NET platform is based on web services, thereby making it easy for components written in Visual Basic to be deployed as web services and consumed by web services written using IBM Visual Age.

This convergence of factors will enable the same kind of network effect that allowed HTML to quickly become the de facto standard for sharing information over the web. Previous distributed computing technologies such as CORBA and DCOM never had the benefit of unanimous acceptance.

Web Services in Action

The best thing about web services is the ability to build cool distributed applications for a fraction of the cost of previous approaches. Here are some example uses of web services in action:

Internet/B2B	Galileo, a leader in travel reservations, provides access to its computer systems via web services. This allows travel agency computers to make reservations using SOAP from anywhere in the world without the expense of older technologies such as Electronic Data Interchange (EDI). In addition, Galileo is opening its systems to cell phones and other devices that can access web services.

Internet/B2C	Microsoft HailStorm allows a consumer to create a personal web service that resides in a secure data center and holds their personal data and files. The consumer maintains control of the access privileges to each piece of data, and can change them at will. By standardizing the XML format of this personal information and allowing access via SOAP, third parties can learn about consumers and provide better service. For example, a hotel could use SOAP to query your personal web service residing in the data center, find out your favorite newspaper, and deliver it to your hotel room without ever bothering you with questions.
Intranet	A large manufacturing company registers web services for its global factory control systems in a private UDDI registry. Internal applications find and use these services for accessing and orchestrating the manufacturing process. In addition, some web services are exposed to enable seamless integration with remote third-party systems.
Local Area Network	A startup company that creates medical imaging software decides to build its next-generation system using web services. Even though most hospitals will run the system on a LAN, basing the communications on SOAP allows the system to be extended to run between hospital networks or even on the Internet. In addition, it allows third-party platforms such as Microsoft .NET to interface to the system without the need for complex protocol converters or gateways.

Although the move to open distributed systems holds a lot of promise, there are a host of associated challenges. The next section discusses some of them.

Challenges

For web services to succeed in the Internet environment, there are many technical challenges to be met. Here are some of the issues:

Reliability	Some web service hosts will be more reliable than others. How can this reliability be measured and described? What happens when a web service host goes offline temporarily? Do you locate and use an alternative service hosted by a different vendor, or do you wait around for the original one to return? How do you know which vendors to trust?
Security	Some web services will be publicly available and unsecured, but most business-related services will use encrypted communications with authentication. It is likely that HTTP over Secured Sockets Layer (SSL) will provide basic security, but individual services will need a higher level of granularity. How does a web service authenticate users? Do services need to be able to provide security on a per-operation basis? If you sign up with a vendor that provides services around the world, how do these services learn about your security privileges?
Discovery	UDDI is the standard that address dynamic discovery of web services. It is a young standard that will probably require several iterations before it is becomes an industrial strength web services matchmaker.
Transactions	Traditional transaction systems use a two-phase commit approach—all of the participating resources are gathered and locked until the entire transaction can take place, at which they are finally released. This approach works fine in a closed environment where transactions are short-lived, but doesn't work well in an open environment where transactions can span hours or even days. Microsoft supports an alternative scheme, called compensating transactions, in its new XLANG system for distributed business processes. Should this kind of transaction be integrated into web services? If so, what is the overlap between this approach and proposed standards like XAML, an XML markup language for supporting traditional transactions?
Scalability	Since it is possible to expose existing component systems like Enterprise JavaBeans (EJB) as web services, it should be possible to leverage the load balancing and other scalability mechanisms that already exist. Or are there unforeseen stumbling blocks along this path? Does there need to be a new kind of "web services" application server?

Manageability	What kinds of mechanisms are required for managing a highly distributed system? Because the properties of a system are a function of the properties of its parts, do the managers of various web services need to coordinate in a particular way? And is it possible to "outsource" the management of web services to other web services? How do you charge for web services? Will the dominant model be subscription based, or pay as you go?
Testing	When a system is comprised of many web services whose location and qualities are potentially dynamic, testing and debugging takes on a whole new dimension. How do you achieve predictable response times? How do you debug web services that can come from different vendors, hosted in different environments and operating systems?

It all sounds very daunting, until you realize that systems that solve these problems already exist. Two such examples are human society and biological organisms. Both exhibit the following properties:

- Fault tolerant
- Massively parallel
- Distributed
- Well organized
- Self-repairing
- Designed in a layered fashion
- Designed out of simple components

By taking the lead from these examples, it should be possible to create a society of web services where components collaborate to achieve their own individual goals. You can easily imagine a networked marketplace where web services rent themselves out to the highest bidder. Mojo Nation is an open source project that takes exactly that approach.

A Science Fiction Kind of Future?

I'd like to finish up this chapter with a science-fiction story that had a great impact on me when I was a boy. The name of the TV series was "Blake's 7", a weekly show that chronicled the adventures of Blake and his six crewmembers as they whizzed around the galaxy in a futuristic spacecraft. ZEN, the artificially intelligent ship's computer, particularly impressed me. It was large like a mainframe, had a deep resonant voice, and was able to perform many duties including running the ship and getting Blake out of more than one sticky situation.

In one episode, Blake and his crew landed on a largely deserted planet and found an old man with a grizzly beard hiding in a cave. The man was a bit of a nutcase, muttering to himself that the bad guys were trying to capture him to steal his treasure. Under one arm he was carrying a small transparent box that seemed to have no great value.

Intrigued, Blake transported him back to the spaceship, and soon learned that the small box was, in fact, the most powerful computer ever built. Apparently, the old man was a computer wizard who had designed the chips that were part of every computer in the galaxy. Secretly, the man put a subspace transceiver into each chip, allowing them to communicate privately over large distances. He built the system so that only one computer, which he called ORAC, had the key to unlock this capability. ORAC was the computer in the transparent box, and when you pressed the on button, ORAC was able to tap into the combined power of all the computers in the galaxy (see Figure 1.17).

The thing that excited me was that tiny ORAC was much smarter than big ZEN because of the way it was designed. Rather than having all of its processing power in one place, its resources were millions of small chips, loosely coupled via a subspace network. That episode greatly influenced the way that I think about computers systems, and convinced me that other systems that adopt the same design approach, such as biological organisms, were a great place to learn about how to build powerful distributed systems.

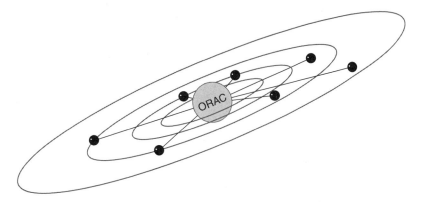

FIGURE 1.17
ORAC leveraged the power of the galactic network

The same pattern seems to occur continually. Smaller mammals replaced large dinosaurs. Client-server systems are replacing mainframes. Each generation keeps getting smaller and smarter.

I think that web services will catalyze a new form of distributed computing, more fluid and dynamic than previous generations, that will take advantage of the billions of devices that are about to inhabit the earth.

Maybe ORAC is not so far away.

Summary

In this chapter, we took a brief tour of distributed computing and saw how web services are a natural successor to technologies such as CORBA and DCOM. In a nutshell, software services that are language, platform, and location independent are destined to inherit the earth.

We also covered SOAP, WSDL, and UDDI, the standards that form the technical underpinning of web services, and discussed the challenges that lie ahead for the mass adoption of the technology.

In the next chapter, I'll show you how to build your own web services and invoke them across the Internet. I'll also show you how to manage and invoke web services from your web browser.

Quiz

- Fill in the blanks: Web Services are software services that are ___, ___, and ___ independent.
- What does SOAP stand for and what is its main purpose?
- What transport layers support web services?
- Why do web services use XML for representing messages?
- What does WSDL stand for and what is its main purpose?
- What does UDDI stand for and what is its main purpose?
- How is a web service exception represented?
- Which companies support web services?
- Why is web services particular good for B2B applications?
- What is "Blake's 7"?

Exercises

1. Browse the web and make a list of all the products that currently support web services.
2. Make a prediction of what distributed computing technology will come *after* web services.
3. Debate whether web services would be better based on a binary message format instead of XML.
4. Predict the kinds of applications that will have the highest early adoption rate of web services.

Hands-On
Web Services

2

Now that we've covered the basics, it's time to put the ideas into action.

This chapter guides you through the creation of a few simple web services that you can run on your own computer or across the Internet. It also shows how you can use a web browser to manage and invoke web services, and introduces common practices such as aggregation and passing XML between services.

It's particularly fun if you can team up with a friend and invoke web services between your home computers.

Your First Web Service

The first hands-on example is a simple currency exchange service that returns the conversion rate between two countries. The Java interface for this service is straightforward, and defines methods for setting and getting the current value in U.S. dollars of a particular country's currency as well as a method for obtaining the exchange rate between two countries' currencies.

Here is the source code for the IExchange interface.

wsbook\src\book\soap\IExchange.java

```
package book.soap;

/**
 * An interface for getting exchange rates.
 */
public interface IExchange
   {
   /**
    * Set the value, in US dollars, of the specified currency.
    * @param country The country.
    * @param value The value in US dollars.
    */
   void setValue( String country, double value );

   /**
    * Return the value of the specified currency.
    * @param country The country.
    * @return The value in US dollars.
    * @throws ExchangeException If the country is not recognized.
    */
   double getValue( String country ) throws ExchangeException;

   /**
    * Return the exchange rate between two countries.
    * @param country1 The country to convert from.
    * @param country2 The country to convert to.
    * @return The exchange rate.
    * @throws ExchangeException If either country is not recognized.
    */
   double getRate( String country1, String country2 ) throws
ExchangeException;
   }
```

The Exchange class is a simple implementation of the `IExchange` interface that stores currency values in a Hashtable.

wsbook\src\book\soap\Exchange.java

```
package book.soap;

import java.util.Hashtable;

/**
 * Simple implementation of IExchange.
 */
public class Exchange implements IExchange
   {
   Hashtable values = new Hashtable(); // in US dollars

   public void setValue( String country, double value )
      {
      values.put( country, new Double( value ) );
      }

   public double getValue( String country )
      throws ExchangeException
      {
      Double value = (Double) values.get( country );

      if( value == null )
         throw new ExchangeException( "country " + country + " not
recognized" );

      return value.doubleValue();
      }

   public double getRate( String country1, String country2 )
      throws ExchangeException
      {
      return getValue( country1 ) / getValue( country2 );
      }
   }
```

Now that we've got the implementation class ready, it's time to publish it for use by SOAP clients. The API for doing this varies between web services platforms, so this chapter shows you how to do it using GLUE and later chapters show you how to do it with Microsoft .NET and BEA WebLogic.

There are two key GLUE classes for building and deploying web services. The first is `Registry`, which includes static methods for publishing web services and binding to them.

publish(String path, Object object)	Publish the object to the specified path, exporting all of the object's public methods.
publish(String path, Class interface)	Publish the object to the specified path, exporting methods in the specified interface.
publish(String path, Class[] interfaces)	Publish the object to the specified path, exporting methods in the specified interfaces.
bind(String path, Class interface)	Return a proxy to the service described by the specified path and that implements the specified interface type. The path can be the local name of the service or the URL of its WSDL file.
unpublish(String path)	Unpublish the object from the specified path.

The second key class is HTTP, which provides static methods for starting up an in-process web server that can accept incoming SOAP requests:

startup(String path)	Start a web server on the specified path.
shutdown()	Shut down any web servers that were started using startup().

Because starting a web server causes some threads to be spawned, a program that calls HTTP.startup() will not terminate until HTTP.shutdown() is called.

The following program starts up a web server on port 8004 of the local host to accept messages arriving on /soap. It then uses Registry.publish() to publish the initialized Exchange object with the name "exchange". Note that the server does not exit when the last line is reached, because the web server has threads running and Java does not halt until all threads have completed.

wsbook\src\book\soap\ExchangeServer.java

```
package book.soap;

import electric.registry.Registry;
import electric.server.http.HTTP;

public class ExchangeServer
  {
  public static void main( String[] args )
    throws Exception
    {
    // start a web server on port 8004, accept messages via /soap
    HTTP.startup( "http://localhost:8004/soap" );

    // initialize an instance of Exchange
    Exchange exchange = new Exchange();
    exchange.setValue( "usa", 1 );
    exchange.setValue( "japan", 0.4 );

    // publish an instance of Exchange
    Registry.publish( "exchange", exchange );
    }
  }
```

The client program binds to the web service by invoking `Registry.bind()` with the path to its WSDL file. GLUE dynamically generates WSDL for the services that it hosts—if an incoming request for a file has a .wsdl extension, it sees if the file name matches that the path of a local service. If this is the case, GLUE examines the local web service, generates and caches its WSDL description, and returns the WSDL file to the requestor. WSDL is described in more detail in the next chapter.

Because Java is a statically typed language, the proxy that is returned by the binding operation must be cast to the interface of the appropriate type. Once the proxy is obtained, the client uses it to invoke the service as if it were a local Java object.

wsbook\src\book\soap\ExchangeClient.java

```
package book.soap;

import electric.registry.Registry;

public class ExchangeClient
  {
  public static void main( String[] args )
```

```
    throws Exception
    {
    // bind to web service whose WSDL is at the specified URL
    String url = "http://localhost:8004/soap/exchange.wsdl";
    IExchange exchange = (IExchange) Registry.bind( url,
IExchange.class );

    // invoke the web service as if it was a local java object
    double rate = exchange.getRate( "usa", "japan" );
    System.out.println( "usa/japan exchange rate = " + rate );
    }
  }
```

To run the example, execute the ExchangeServer program in one window and the ExchangeClient program in another window. Here is the output for ExchangeServer:

```
> java book.soap.ExchangeServer
GLUE 1.2 (c) 2001 The Mind Electric
startup server on http://199.174.17.98:8004/soap
```

Here is the output for ExchangeClient:

```
> java book.soap.ExchangeClient
usa/japan exchange rate = 2.5

> _
```

To run the same example across the Internet, simply replace the URL in the ExchangeClient with the URL of the remote server.

To see the WSDL file for the web service, type http://localhost:8004/soap/exchange.wsdl into your web browser.

Sniffing SOAP

It's interesting and instructive to see SOAP messages as they fly back and forth between programs. To enable a trace of SOAP messages, execute the previous example with the electric.logging property set to "SOAP". For example, to run the server with SOAP logging enabled, type the following:

```
> java -Delectric.logging="SOAP" book.soap.ExchangeServer
GLUE 1.2 (c) 2001 The Mind Electric
startup server on http://199.174.17.98:8004/soap
```

To run the client with SOAP logging enabled, type:

```
> java -Delectric.logging="SOAP" book.soap.ExchangeClient
```

You should see the following kind of client-side log. The server-side log is similar.

```
> java -Delectric.logging="SOAP" book.soap.ExchangeClient
LOG.SOAP: request to http://199.174.17.11:8004/soap/exchange
  <?xml version='1.0' encoding='UTF-8'?>
  <soap:Envelope
    xmlns:xsi='http://www.w3.org/2001/XMLSchema-instance'
    xmlns:xsd='http://www.w3.org/2001/XMLSchema'
    xmlns:soap='http://schemas.xmlsoap.org/soap/envelope/'
    xmlns:soapenc='http://schemas.xmlsoap.org/soap/encoding/'
    soap:encodingStyle='http://schemas.xmlsoap.org/soap/encoding/'>
    <soap:Body>
      <n:getRate xmlns:n='http://tempuri.org/book.soap.Exchange'>
        <country1 xsi:type='xsd:string'>usa</country1>
        <country2 xsi:type='xsd:string'>japan</country2>
      </n:getRate>
    </soap:Body>
  </soap:Envelope>

LOG.SOAP: response from http://199.174.17.11:8004/soap/exchange
  <?xml version='1.0' encoding='UTF-8'?>
  <soap:Envelope
    xmlns:xsi='http://www.w3.org/2001/XMLSchema-instance'
    xmlns:xsd='http://www.w3.org/2001/XMLSchema'
    xmlns:soap='http://schemas.xmlsoap.org/soap/envelope/'
    xmlns:soapenc='http://schemas.xmlsoap.org/soap/encoding/'
    soap:encodingStyle='http://schemas.xmlsoap.org/soap/encoding/'>
    <soap:Body>
      <n:getRateResponse xmlns:n='http://tempuri.org/book.soap.Exchange'>
        <Result xsi:type='xsd:double'>2.5</Result>
      </n:getRateResponse>
    </soap:Body>
  </soap:Envelope>

usa/japan exchange rate = 2.5

> _
```

The `xsi:type` attributes indicate the types of each argument. In this case, the input arguments are both strings, and the return value is a double. More detail about XML types, including information about how to pass objects between web services, is presented in Chapter 4.

To see what a SOAP exception looks like on the wire, run the previous example but with a nonexistent country like `"spam"` as a parameter to `getRate()`. To see HTTP logging as well as SOAP, set the electric.logging property to `"HTTP, SOAP"`.

Browsing Web Services

When you're first getting used to web services, it's handy to be able to browse, invoke, and create them from a web browser. To see how this is possible, first run the ExchangeServer example on http://localhost:8004/soap by typing:

```
> java book.soap.ExchangeServer
```

Then start a GLUE console by typing:

```
> console
```

This command starts a console application on port 8100 by default. Then type http://localhost:8100 into your web browser. Figure 2.1 is the console start page.

To log in to a GLUE host and view its contents, type the URL of the host into the HOME field and click Home. This takes you to the home page for the host, which lists its endpoints and its services. In this example, type http://localhost:8004/soap. Figure 2.2 illustrates what comes up.

On the top right hand side of the page are two links, START and HOME. START takes you back to the console start page, and HOME takes you back to the home page of the host that you're currently logged in to.

The exchange service is the one that was published by the ExchangeServer, and the system/admin service is a web service that every GLUE host contains that enables remote administration.

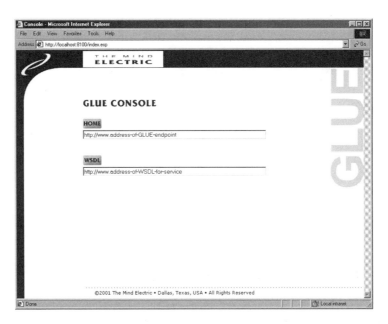

FIGURE 2.1
The console start page

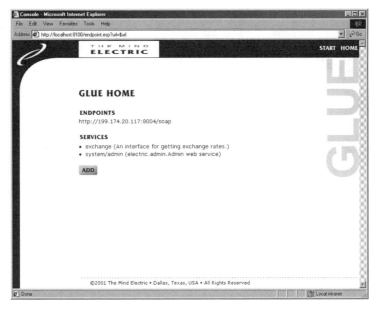

FIGURE 2.2
The host's home page

Click the "exchange" link under the Services heading to get a description of
the web service (see Figure 2.3), including its endpoint URL, WSDL URL,
Java class type, and list of available methods. The web services descriptions
are extracted automatically from the source of the IExchange interface.

The MODE field refers to the activation mode of the web service. Most
SOAP containers support three activation modes:

Application	All requests are delivered to a single shared object. This is the most common mode, and is the same as the default activation mode used by CORBA and Remote Method Invocation (RMI).
Session	Creates an object to handle each session and destroys the object when the session is over. If ten sessions are running at once, there will be ten instances of the object, one for each concurrent session. A single logical service can map to more than one Java object.
Request	Creates an object to handle each request and destroys the object at the end of the request.

I'll show you how to change the activation mode later in this section.

FIGURE 2.3
The web service description

To see more information about a method, click on its link. The console will display its name, inputs, outputs, and SOAP Action value (see Figure 2.4). The endpoint field is hyperlinked back to its web service page. The input and output types are shown as Java types.

To invoke the method, enter values for each of the input fields and then click SEND. The result is displayed in Figure 2.5. If the method does not have a return type, null is displayed.

You can invoke the service again by repeating this process. Depending on the location of the web service, it may take a while for the response to be displayed. The bottom of your browser window normally displays an indicator that the console is waiting for an HTTP response.

To add a service, go back to the console start page by clicking the upper-right-hand HOME link. Then click ADD. You'll be prompted to enter the description, Uniform Resource Name (URN), class and mode of the web service to be added (see Figure 2.6). In this example, enter:

- Description = another exchange service
- URN = exchange2
- Class = book.soap.Exchange
- Mode = application

FIGURE 2.4
Web method information

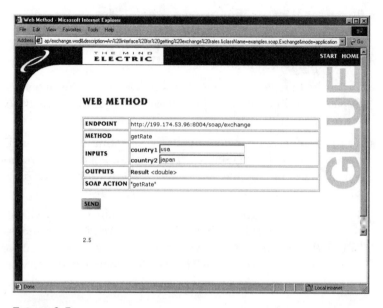

FIGURE 2.5
Invoking a method

FIGURE 2.6
Adding a service

Then click SAVE.

Assuming that everything went all right, you should see Figure 2.7, which lists the properties of the new web service.

To edit the service, click EDIT and change fields to their new values. In the example in Figure 2.8, change the mode to Request, which means that a new instance of the service will be created for every invocation. Then press SAVE.

When you go back to the home page, you should see the new service in the Services listing (see Figure 2.9).

To delete a service, go to its description page and press DEL.

In the WSDL section, I'll show you how to use the console to browse and invoke third-party web services. In the meantime, let's take a look at a common use of web services, which is to aggregate other web services.

FIGURE 2.7
Properties of the new web service

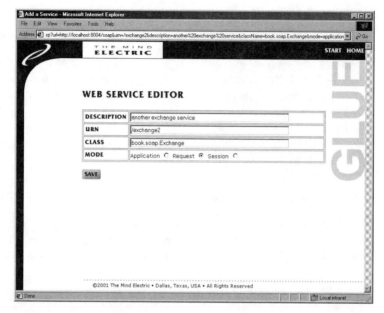

FIGURE 2.8
Editing the service

FIGURE 2.9
The new home page

Aggregation

Web services are building blocks for distributed applications, so it's common for a web service to aggregate and orchestrate other web services. For example, a web service could provide a high-level set of travel features by orchestrating lower-level web services for car rental, air travel, and hotels.

Because a web service can be accessed through a regular Java interface, it is straightforward to create a higher-level service that accesses lower level services as if they were local objects.

Figure 2.10 illustrates this approach by creating an International Trader service that uses a Trader service and an Exchange service to buy shares and return the cost in a specified currency. Of course, users of the International Trader service do not know or care that it is a service aggregator.

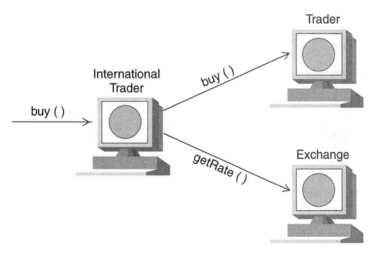

FIGURE 2.10
International Trader aggregates a Trader and an Exchange

Here is the interface for the International Trader service.

wsbook\src\book\aggregation\IInterationalTrader.java

```
package book.aggregation;

import book.soap.TradeException;
import book.soap.ExchangeException;

/**
 * An interface for buying shares using any currency.
 */
public interface IInternationalTrader
  {
  /**
    * Purchase the specified stock.
    * @param quantity The number of shares to purchase.
    * @param symbol The ticker symbol of the company.
    * @param country The country.
    * @throws TradeException If the symbol is not recognized.
    * @throws ExchangeException If the country is not recognized.
    * @return The cost of the purchase in the currency of the country.
    */
  float buy( int quantity, String symbol, String country )
    throws TradeException, ExchangeException;
  }
```

The InternationalTrader class is an implementation of the IInternation-alTrader interface that uses the trader and exchange services passed in at construction time. When the buy() method is executed, it first invokes buy() on the trader service, then invokes getRate() on the exchange service, and finally returns the calculated result. Because interfaces are passed in, the implementations of these services could be local or a web service anywhere in the world.

wsbook\src\book\aggregation\InternationalTrader.java

```
package book.aggregation;

import book.soap.ITrader;
import book.soap.IExchange;
import book.soap.TradeException;
import book.soap.ExchangeException;

/**
 * Implementation of IInternationalTrader.
 */
public class InternationalTrader implements IInternationalTrader
```

```
  {
  ITrader trader;
  IExchange exchange;

  public InternationalTrader( ITrader trader, IExchange exchange )
    {
    this.trader = trader;
    this.exchange = exchange;
    }

  public float buy( int quantity, String symbol, String country )
    throws TradeException, ExchangeException
    {
    System.out.println( "invoke trader.buy( " + quantity + ", " +
symbol + " )" );
    float cost = trader.buy( quantity, symbol );
    System.out.println( "  ... returns " + cost );

    System.out.println( "invoke exchange.getRate( usa, " + country +
" )" );
    double rate = exchange.getRate( "usa", country );
    System.out.println( "  ... returns " + rate );

    float result = cost * (float) rate;
    System.out.println( "return final result " + result );
    return result;
    }
  }
```

The server program that hosts the International Trader service runs on port 8005 and uses the Trader and Exchange services that are presumed to be running on local ports 8003 and 8004, respectively.

wsbook\src\book\aggregation\InternationalServer.java

```
package book.aggregation;

import electric.registry.Registry;
import electric.server.http.HTTP;
import book.soap.ITrader;
import book.soap.IExchange;

public class InternationalServer
  {
  public static void main( String[] args )
    throws Exception
    {
    // start a web server on port 8005, accept messages via /soap
    HTTP.startup( "http://localhost:8005/soap" );

    // bind to trader service
```

```
    String traderURL = "http://localhost:8003/soap/trader.wsdl";
    ITrader trader = (ITrader) Registry.bind( traderURL,
ITrader.class );

    // bind to exchange service
    String exchangeURL = "http://localhost:8004/soap/exchange.wsdl";
    IExchange exchange = (IExchange) Registry.bind( exchangeURL,
IExchange.class );

    // publish an instance of InternationalTrader
    InternationalTrader iTrader = new InternationalTrader( trader,
exchange );
    Registry.publish( "i-trader", iTrader );
    }
  }
```

The client program binds to the International Trader service and invokes it just like any other web service. The fact that the International Trader service is aggregating other services is hidden from the outside world.

wsbook\src\book\aggregation\InternationalClient.java

```
package book.aggregation;

import electric.registry.Registry;

public class InternationalClient
  {
  public static void main( String[] args )
    throws Exception
    {
    // bind to international trader service
    String url = "http://localhost:8005/soap/i-trader.wsdl";
    IInternationalTrader iTrader = (IInternationalTrader)
Registry.bind( url, IInternationalTrader.class );

    // invoke the web service as if it was a local java object
    float yenCost = iTrader.buy( 40, "IBM", "japan" );
    System.out.println( "40 shares of IBM in yen = " + yenCost );
    }
  }
```

To run the example, execute the TraderServer, ExchangeServer, and InternationalServer programs in separate windows. Then run the InterationalClient program in another window.

You should see the following output from TraderServer.

```
> java book.soap.TraderServer
GLUE 1.2 (c) 2001 The Mind Electric
startup server on http://199.174.53.96:8003/soap
```

Here's the output from ExchangeServer.

```
> java book.soap.ExchangeServer
GLUE 1.2 (c) 2001 The Mind Electric
startup server on http://199.174.53.96:8004/soap
```

Here's the output from InternationalServer, which displays the partial results from the services that it aggregates.

```
> java book.aggregation.InternationalServer
GLUE 1.2 (c) 2001 The Mind Electric
startup server on http://199.174.53.96:8005/soap
invoke trader.buy( 40, IBM )
   ... returns 4696.0
invoke exchange.getRate( usa, japan )
   ... returns 2.5
return final result 11740.0
```

Finally, here's the output from InternationalClient:

```
> java book.aggregation.InternationalClient
40 shares of IBM in yen = 11740.0

> _
```

Exchanging XML Documents

It is often convenient to send XML documents between web services. One simple and portable way to do this is to convert the XML into a String or byte array on the client, send it via a String argument, and then convert it back to an XML document on the server.

There are several toolkits that simplify the parsing and manipulation of XML documents. This section uses Electric XML, which is included in GLUE, but the same technique applies to other libraries such as DOM, JDOM, and DOM4J.

In the following example, a client sends an XML order form to a remote Store object for processing. Here is the IStore interface, which declares a single method that accepts an XML document as a String.

wsbook\src\book\xml\IStore.java

```
package book.xml;

public interface IStore
   {
   void process( String xmlOrder );
   }
```

The Store class is a simple implementation of the IStore interface that creates an XML document from the incoming String and then displays the document together with its customer element.

wsbook\src\book\xml\Store.java

```
package book.xml;

import electric.xml.*;

public class Store implements IStore
   {
   public void process( String xmlOrder )
      {
      try
         {
         Document document = new Document( xmlOrder );
         System.out.println( "got XML document:\n" );
         System.out.println( document );
         String customer = document.getRoot().getTextString( "customer" );
         System.out.println( "customer = " + customer );
         }
      catch( ParseException exception )
         {
         exception.printStackTrace();
         }
      }
   }
```

The XMLServer program publishes an instance of the Store web service.

wsbook\src\book\xml\XMLServer.java

```
package book.xml;

import electric.registry.Registry;
import electric.server.http.HTTP;
```

```
public class XMLServer
   {
   public static void main( String[] args )
     throws Exception
     {
     // start a web server on port 8004, accept messages via /glue
     HTTP.startup( "http://localhost:8004/soap" );

     // publish an instance of Store
     Registry.publish( "store", new Store() );
     }
   }
```

The XMLClient program creates an XML document and sends it to the Store for processing. Document and Element are classes from the Electric XML library which is part of the GLUE platform.

wsbook\src\book\xml\XMLClient.java

```
package book.xml;

import electric.registry.Registry;
import electric.xml.*;

public class XMLClient
   {
   public static void main( String[] args )
     throws Exception
     {
     // bind to web service whose WSDL is at the specified URL
     String url = "http://localhost:8004/soap/store.wsdl";
     IStore store = (IStore) Registry.bind( url, IStore.class );

     // create document to send
     Document document = new Document();
     document.addChild( new XMLDecl( "1.0", "UTF-8" ) );
     Element root = document.setRoot( "order" );
     root.addElement( "quantity" ).setText( "144" );
     root.addElement( "product" ).setText( "wall clock" );
     root.addElement( "customer" ).setText( "graham glass" );
     String xml = document.toString();

     System.out.println( "send XML document " + xml );
     store.process( xml );
     }
   }
```

To run the example, execute the XMLServer program in one window and the XMLClient in another window. Here is the server output:

```
> java book.xml.XMLServer
GLUE 1.2 (c) 2001 The Mind Electric
startup server on http://199.174.53.96:8004/soap
got XML document:

<?xml version='1.0' encoding='UTF-8'?>
<order>
  <quantity>144</quantity>
  <product>wall clock</product>
  <customer>graham glass</customer>
</order>
customer = graham glass
```

Here is the client output:

```
> java book.xml.XMLClient
send XML document <?xml version='1.0' encoding='UTF-8'?>
<order>
  <quantity>144</quantity>
  <product>wall clock</product>
  <customer>graham glass</customer>
</order>

> _
```

The technique of passing XML documents as arguments to web services allows you the flexibility of sending arbitrary structures between applications without having to know their contents in advance.

Summary

In this chapter, we used a few simple APIs to create and host a web service in a SOAP server, then invoke it from a SOAP client. A browser was used to list the contents of a SOAP server, invoke one of its services, and add a service.

We also looked at an example of web service aggregation, and a technique for passing XML documents between applications.

In the next chapter, we'll take a look at WSDL and see how it enables client-side bindings for third-party web services to be created automatically.

Quiz

- What does XSD stand for?
- Describe the technique of aggregation.
- Why might you choose to pass an XML document using a byte array instead of a String?

Exercises

1. Brainstorm a set of additional features that you think a web services console would benefit from.
2. Before reading Chapter 4, think about how you would send objects between applications.
3. Download and try out some other SOAP platforms (see the reference section for some links).
4. How can aggregators cope when one of their web services components dies?

Web Services Description Language (WSDL)

3

WSDL is an XML grammar for describing the characteristics of a web service. WSDL files can be used by development tools for creating interfaces to web services, and by run-time systems for dynamically binding to web services. WSDL is not intended for direct consumption by developers, although it is useful and interesting to understand the details of its grammar.

This chapter examines WSDL in detail, and shows how its XML grammar allows the many facets of a web service to be expressed. It also demonstrates how WSDL can be used to generate client-side bindings for third-party web services, greatly simplifying the process of integrating remote web services into an application.

Let's start by taking a look at a WSDL file.

The Anatomy of WSDL

Every deployed web service has an associated URL which points to its WSDL file, which is either generated statically using a development tool or dynamically from the hosted web service. By default, GLUE generates WSDL dynamically, so to see the WSDL for an instance of the Exchange web service from Chapter 2, run the ExchangeServer and then type http://localhost:8004/soap/exchange.wsdl into your web browser.

You should see the screen in Figure 3.1.

Internet Explorer (IE) automatically colors and structures XML content, which makes following the sections of WSDL a little easier.

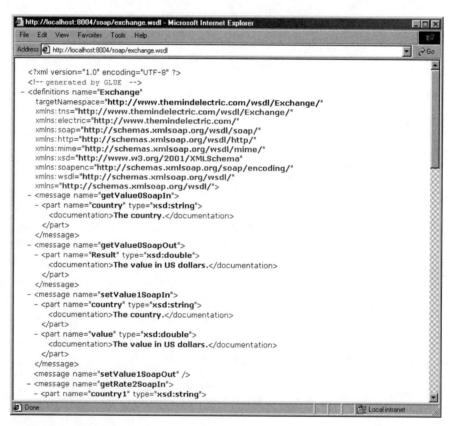

FIGURE 3.1
WDSL as an Exchange web service instance

For convenience, here are the complete contents of the http://local-host:8004/soap/exchange.wsdl file. The individual sections are discussed following the listing.

http://localhost:8004/soap/exchange.wsdl

```xml
<?xml version="1.0" encoding="UTF-8" ?>
<!-- generated by GLUE -->

<definitions
  name="Exchange"
  targetNamespace="http://www.themindelectric.com/wsdl/Exchange/"
  xmlns:tns="http://www.themindelectric.com/wsdl/Exchange/"
  xmlns:electric="http://www.themindelectric.com/"
  xmlns:soap="http://schemas.xmlsoap.org/wsdl/soap/"
  xmlns:http="http://schemas.xmlsoap.org/wsdl/http/"
  xmlns:mime="http://schemas.xmlsoap.org/wsdl/mime/"
  xmlns:xsd="http://www.w3.org/2001/XMLSchema"
  xmlns:soapenc="http://schemas.xmlsoap.org/soap/encoding/"
  xmlns:wsdl="http://schemas.xmlsoap.org/wsdl/"
  xmlns="http://schemas.xmlsoap.org/wsdl/">

  <message name="getValue0SoapIn">
    <part name="country" type="xsd:string">
      <documentation>The country.</documentation>
    </part>
  </message>

  <message name="getValue0SoapOut">
    <part name="Result" type="xsd:double">
      <documentation>The value in US dollars.</documentation>
    </part>
  </message>

  <message name="setValue1SoapIn">
    <part name="country" type="xsd:string">
      <documentation>The country.</documentation>
    </part>
    <part name="value" type="xsd:double">
      <documentation>The value in US dollars.</documentation>
    </part>
  </message>

  <message name="setValue1SoapOut" />

  <message name="getRate2SoapIn">
    <part name="country1" type="xsd:string">
      <documentation>The country to convert from.</documentation>
    </part>
    <part name="country2" type="xsd:string">
      <documentation>The country to convert to.</documentation>
    </part>
  </message>
```

```
<message name="getRate2SoapOut">
  <part name="Result" type="xsd:double">
    <documentation>The exchange rate.</documentation>
  </part>
</message>

<portType name="ExchangeSoap">
  <operation name="getValue" parameterOrder="country">
    <documentation>
      Return the value of the specified currency.
    </documentation>
    <input name="getValue0SoapIn" message="tns:getValue0SoapIn" />
    <output name="getValue0SoapOut" message="tns:getValue0SoapOut"
/>
  </operation>

  <operation name="setValue" parameterOrder="country value">
    <documentation>
      Set the value, in US dollars, of the specified currency.
    </documentation>
    <input name="setValue1SoapIn" message="tns:setValue1SoapIn" />
    <output name="setValue1SoapOut" message="tns:setValue1SoapOut" />
  </operation>

  <operation name="getRate" parameterOrder="country1 country2">
    <documentation>
      Return the exchange rate between two countries.
    </documentation>
    <input name="getRate2SoapIn" message="tns:getRate2SoapIn" />
    <output name="getRate2SoapOut" message="tns:getRate2SoapOut" />
  </operation>
</portType>

<binding name="ExchangeSoap" type="tns:ExchangeSoap">
  <soap:binding
    style="rpc"
    transport="http://schemas.xmlsoap.org/soap/http" />

  <operation name="getValue">
    <soap:operation soapAction="getValue" style="rpc" />
    <input name="getValue0SoapIn">
      <soap:body
        use="encoded"
        namespace="http://tempuri.org/book.soap.Exchange"
        encodingStyle="http://schemas.xmlsoap.org/soap/encoding/" />
    </input>
    <output name="getValue0SoapOut">
      <soap:body
        use="encoded"
        namespace="http://tempuri.org/book.soap.Exchange"
        encodingStyle="http://schemas.xmlsoap.org/soap/encoding/" />
    </output>
  </operation>
```

```
   <operation name="setValue">
     <soap:operation soapAction="setValue" style="rpc" />
     <input name="setValue1SoapIn">
       <soap:body
         use="encoded"
         namespace="http://tempuri.org/book.soap.Exchange"
         encodingStyle="http://schemas.xmlsoap.org/soap/encoding/" />
     </input>
     <output name="setValue1SoapOut">
       <soap:body
         use="encoded"
         namespace="http://tempuri.org/book.soap.Exchange"
         encodingStyle="http://schemas.xmlsoap.org/soap/encoding/" />
     </output>
   </operation>

   <operation name="getRate">
     <soap:operation soapAction="getRate" style="rpc" />
     <input name="getRate2SoapIn">
       <soap:body
         use="encoded"
         namespace="http://tempuri.org/book.soap.Exchange"
         encodingStyle="http://schemas.xmlsoap.org/soap/encoding/" />
     </input>
     <output name="getRate2SoapOut">
     <soap:body
       use="encoded"
       namespace="http://tempuri.org/book.soap.Exchange"
       encodingStyle="http://schemas.xmlsoap.org/soap/encoding/" />
     </output>
   </operation>
 </binding>

 <service name="Exchange">
   <documentation>An interface for getting exchange rates.</
documentation>
   <port name="ExchangeSoap" binding="tns:ExchangeSoap">
     <soap:address location="http://199.174.21.187:8004/soap/exchange"
/>
   </port>
 </service>

</definitions>
```

As you can see, WSDL is fairly verbose, and certainly not intended for a human audience. Although it looks quite complex at first glance, it's actually fairly straightforward once you know the purpose of the various sections. Here is an overview of the six main WSDL tags:

\<description\>	This is the top-level section, and contains the definition of one or more services. The \<definitions\> tag is followed by several attributes, including targetNamespace that indicates the XML namespace into which all WSDL definitions are placed. For convenience, a namespace (often called xmlns:tns) is set to the value of targetNamespace.
\<types\>	This optional section contains type declarations for all of the non-built-in data types that the service uses, such as arrays and structures. This example does not use any complex types, and so this section is not present.
\<message\>	A message corresponds to a single piece of information moving between the invoker and the service. A regular round trip method call is modeled as two messages, one for the request and one for the response. Each message can have zero or more parts, and each part can have a name and an optional type. When WSDL describes a Java service, each part maps to an argument of a method call. If a method returns void, the response is an empty message. The name of a message does not have to correspond to the name of a method, and serves only used as a handle when defining operations (see next paragraph).
\<portType\>	A portType corresponds to a set of one or more operations, where an operation defines a specific input/output message sequence. The message attribute of each input/output must correspond to the name of a message that was defined earlier in the WSDL document. If an operation specifies just an input, it is a one-way operation. An output followed by an input is a solicit-response operation, and a single input is a notification. When WSDL describes a Java class, each operation maps to a method and each portType maps to a Java interface or class. An operation can have an optional parameterOrder attribute that lists the names of the input parameters in order.
\<binding\>	A binding corresponds to a portType implemented using a particular protocol such as SOAP or CORBA. The type attribute of the binding must correspond to the name of a portType that was defined earlier in the WSDL document. If a service supports more than one protocol, the WSDL includes a binding for each. In this example, the binding is a SOAP/RPC binding that uses the standard encoding style.

\<service\>	A service is modeled as a collection of ports, where a port represents the availability of a particular binding at a specified endpoint. The binding attribute of a port must correspond to the name of a binding that was defined earlier in the WSDL document. In this example, the service supports a SOAP/RPC binding to the Exchange port type, and is located at http://localhost:8004/soap/exchange.

The real benefit of this rich XML description becomes apparent when you want to use third-party web services. Let's try some out.

Browsing Third-Party Web Services

One of the best sites for third-party web services is http://www.xmethods.net, which acts both as a clearinghouse for web services and an educational resource for developers who want to experiment with web services technology.

If you visit XMethods, you'll see a listing of web services on the home page (see Figure 3.2). Each service has a brief overview, which includes the hosting company, the name of the service, a description, and the web services platform that it's running on.

To see more about a particular service, click its name. To illustrate the power and usefulness of WSDL, we'll click the Delayed Stock Quotes service toward the bottom of the list and use its WSDL to automatically create client-side bindings for the service.

Figure 3.3 illustrates what you should see when you click the Stock Quotes service.

The XMethods service details page contains more information about the web service, including its endpoint URL, the required SOAP Action field, the method namespace, and the list of available methods. In this case, the Stock Quotes service has a single method called `getQuote`.

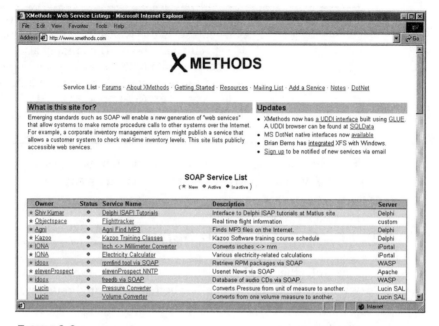

FIGURE 3.2
The XMethods home page

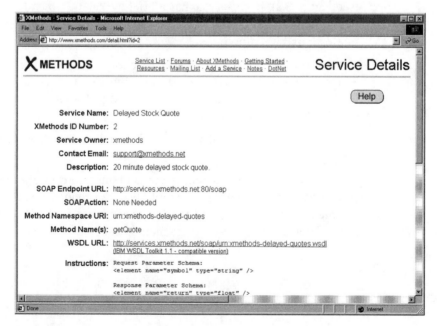

FIGURE 3.3
Delayed stock quotes service

To see its WSDL file, click on the WSDL hyperlink. You should see the screen in Figure 3.4.

As usual, the <definitions> section defines several attributes followed by the <message>, <portType>, <binding>, and <service> sections. Because the service is simple and only uses primitive types, there is no <types> section.

Most web services platforms include tools for browsing and interacting with services based on their WSDL, as well as utilities for creating proxies from the WSDL. To see an example of this, launch the GLUE console and enter the URL that we just looked at into the WSDL window (see Figure 3.5).

Then press WSDL to see an overview of the web service that is described by that WSDL.

With the push of a button, GLUE loaded the WSDL from across the Internet, parsed its XML description, and made the information available through the browser. Figure 3.6 is what you'll see.

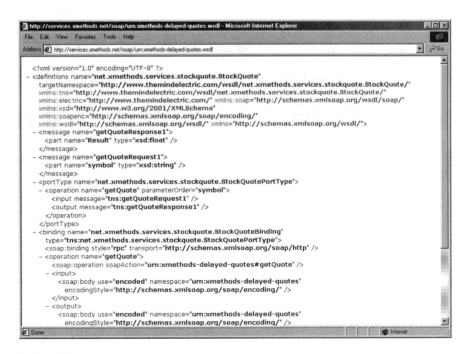

FIGURE 3.4
A WDSL file

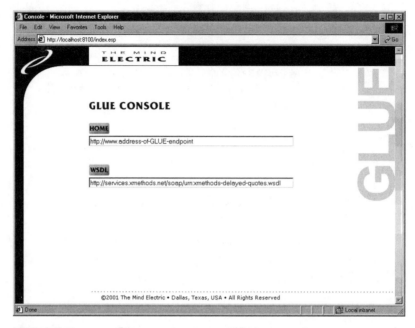

FIGURE 3.5
Tools for browsing

FIGURE 3.6
A web service overview

Because the WSDL contains all the information that is necessary to invoke the web service methods, you can easily invoke the service directly from the browser. Click the getQuote link (Figure 3.7) to see detailed information about the method.

To invoke the method, enter the arguments and press SEND. The result is displayed at the bottom of the page in a separate frame. In this example, I entered IBM and got back a stock price of $112.89.

Depending on Internet conditions, there may be a noticeable delay between pressing the button and seeing the result. The browser status bar generally lets you know that the message is in progress.

Most platforms are able to automatically generate Java interfaces from a WSDL description (see Figure 3.8). For example, if you go back to the main page for the Stock Quote service and press the JAVA button, you'll see a Java interface for the Stock Quote service and a helper class, both of which can be copied and pasted into a Java client. The wsdl2java utility, described in the next section, can generate similar Java bindings from the command line.

FIGURE 3.7
Details of getting a quote

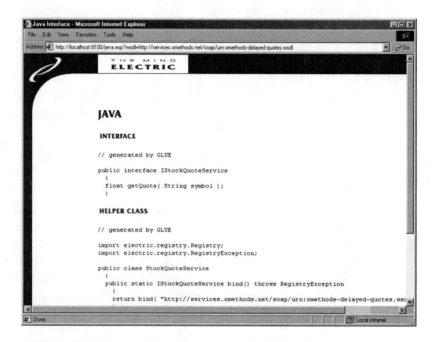

FIGURE 3.8
The Java description

Now that we've seen how WSDL allows tools to browse and invoke third-party web services, let's see how these services can be incorporated into an application.

Consuming Third-Party Web Services

Most web services platforms include a utility for automatically creating client-side access code from a WSDL file. For example, to generate a Java interface and helper class for the Stock Quotes service in the previous section, enter the following wsdl2java command from the wsbook\src\book\wsdl directory, using the -p option to place the code into the book.wsdl package.

```
> wsdl2java http://services.xmethods.net/soap/
urn:xmethods-delayed-quotes.wsdl -p book.wsdl
write file IStockQuoteService.java
write file StockQuoteServiceHelper.java
> _
```

The IStockQuoteService.java interface is a regular Java interface with no coupling to anything that is web-service specific. The name and argument types of each method are extracted automatically from the WSDL file.

wsbook\src\book\wsdl\IStockQuoteService.java

```
// generated by GLUE

package book.wsdl;

public interface IStockQuoteService
  {
  float getQuote( String symbol );
  }
```

The StockQuoteServiceHelper class simplifies access to the remote web service. It defines a couple of static methods, one that returns a proxy to the specific web service, and another that returns a proxy to a similar service but at a different specified location.

wsbook\src\book\wsdl\StockQuoteServiceHelper.java

```
// generated by GLUE

package book.wsdl;

import electric.registry.Registry;
import electric.registry.RegistryException;

public class StockQuoteServiceHelper
  {
  public static IStockQuoteService bind() throws RegistryException
    {
    return bind( "http://services.xmethods.net/soap/urn:xmethods-delayed-
quotes.wsdl" );
    }

  public static IStockQuoteService bind( String url ) throws
RegistryException
    {
    return (IStockQuoteService) Registry.bind( url, IStockQuoteService.class
);
    }
  }
```

To access the Stock Quotes service from an application, call StockQuote-ServiceHelper.bind(). The following client gets an IBM stock quote using this approach.

wsbook\src\book\wsdl\QuoteClient.java

```
package book.wsdl;

public class QuoteClient
  {
  public static void main( String[] args )
    throws Exception
    {
    IStockQuoteService quotes = StockQuoteServiceHelper.bind();
    float ibm = quotes.getQuote( "IBM" );
    System.out.println( "IBM quote is " + ibm );
    }
  }
```

To run the example, execute the QuoteClient program in a window. Here is the output:

```
> java book.wsdl.QuoteClient
IBM quote is 108.18

> _
```

The next chapter includes more complex examples that show how to pass objects to third-party web services.

Modularizing WSDL

WSDL can be modularized for readability and reuse through the use of the <import> statement. For example, you could restructure the WSDL file at the start of this chapter into two separate files, one that represents a service interface and one that represents a service implementation.

WSDL for a service interface contains only <type>, <message>, and <portType> elements. For example, here is a WSDL file that describes the interface for an Exchange service.

http://www.themindelectric.com/wsdl/ExchangeInterface.wsdl

```
<?xml version='1.0' encoding='UTF-8'?>
<definitions
  name='Exchange'
  targetNamespace='http://www.themindelectric.com/wsdl/ExchangeInterface/
'
```

```
...
xmlns='http://schemas.xmlsoap.org/wsdl/'>

<message name='getRateRequest3'>
  <part name='country1' type='xsd:string'>
    <documentation>The country to convert from.</documentation>
  </part>
  ...
</message>
...
<portType name='ExchangeSoap'>
  <operation name='getValue' parameterOrder='country'>
  ...
  </operation>
  ...
</portType>
</definitions>
```

WSDL for a service implementation file includes <binding> and <service> portions. For example, here is a WSDL file that describes the implementation for an Exchange service and imports the previously defined WSDL interface file.

http://www.themindelectric.com/wsdl/Exchange.wsdl

```
<?xml version='1.0' encoding='UTF-8'?>
<definitions
  name='Exchange'
  targetNamespace='http://www.themindelectric.com/wsdl/Exchange/'
  xmlns:tns='http://www.themindelectric.com/wsdl/Exchange/'
  xmlns:ins='http://www.themindelectric.com/wsdl/ExchangeInterface/'
  ...
  xmlns='http://schemas.xmlsoap.org/wsdl/'>

  <import
    location='http://www.themindelectric.com/wsdl/ExchangeInterface.wsdl
    namespace='http://www.themindelectric.com/wsdl/ExchangeInterface/>

  <binding
    name='ExchangeSoap'
    type='ins:ExchangeSoap'>
    ...
  </binding>

  <service name='Exchange>
    <documentation>An interface for exchange rates.</documentation>
    <port
      name='ExchangeSoap'
      binding='tns:ExchangeSoap>
      <soap:address location='http://199.174.18.218:8004/soap/exchange'/>
    </port>
  </service>
</definitions>
```

Most SOAP platforms can interpret <import> statements but do not create WSDL that uses <import> by default. I suspect that over time, use of the <import> statement will become more common.

Summary

In this chapter, we examined the structure of a WSDL file and saw how its rich XML grammar allows client-side bindings to be automatically generated for third-party web services.

We also saw how WSDL can be modularized using the <import> statement.

In the next chapter, we'll take a look at how complex data structures can be passed between web services, allowing objects to be transmitted between applications in a portable manner.

Quiz

- What are the six main XML tags used by WSDL?
- Where is the location of a web service stored in a WSDL file?
- Can WSDL express a CORBA binding?
- Does WSDL define a field that represents quality of service?

Exercises

1. Discuss the benefits of WSDL over CORBA IDL.
2. What kind of information do you think WSDL will include in the future?
3. Design a more compact way to represent the same information as WSDL.
4. Discuss whether WSDL should have been designed to be more readable by developers.
5. Visit XMethods and register one of your own web services.
6. Browse the web and locate other web service registries.

Mapping Between Native Data Structures and XML

The examples so far have sent only primitive data types between services. Now it's time to see how complex data types, such as objects, can be sent between web services in a portable manner.

This chapter describes how complex data types can be mapped to XML for transmission on the wire and how to customize the mapping under special circumstances. The examples include wire dumps that show the SOAP representation of each data type.

All of the examples in this chapter are written in Java. For an example of how objects can be sent using SOAP between Java programs and C# programs, see the .NET chapter (Chapter 8).

Let's start with an overview of the mapping problem from the server and client perspectives.

Overview

Because SOAP messages are XML documents, all data items flowing between endpoints are represented using XML Schema Datatypes (XSD). XSD defines the way that primitive and complex types are represented in XML. Several versions of the XSD specification have been released over the last few years, and most SOAP implementations implement the latest 2001 specification.

It's simple to send primitive data types between web services, because there's a trivial mapping between these types and their XSD equivalents. Things get a bit more complicated when you need to pass objects between web services, because they must be mapped to a language- and platform-neutral XML format (see Figure 4.1).

The mapping process can be viewed from two perspectives:

1. On the *server* side, a component is published as a service using a SOAP container. The WSDL is generated dynamically or using a utility like java2wsdl. The WSDL generator uses some default rules to perform the mapping from the native representation to its associated XML Schema.

2. On the *client* side, a utility like wsdl2java is used to create native language bindings for a web service from its WSDL. The code generator uses some default rules to perform the mapping from an XML Schema to its associated native representation.

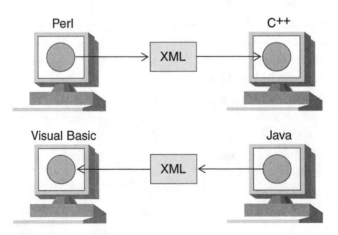

FIGURE 4.1
SOAP uses XML to pass objects between programs of any language

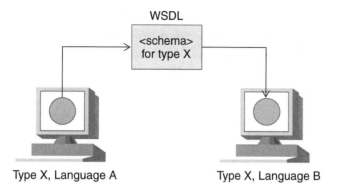

FIGURE 4.2
WSDL contains XML Schema for native types

The same mapping rules are also used at run time to convert native representations to and from their XML equivalents (see Figure 4.2).

Although it's fairly straightforward to convert a simple native representation to XML, there are some complications. For example, if you serialize an object graph into XML, how do you preserve morphology and deal with cyclic references? And how are arrays represented? Fortunately, section 5 of the SOAP specification contains instructions on how to do this, and SOAP operations that utilize this approach are indicated in WSDL with the `use` attribute equal to `encoded`. If a SOAP operation is specified with the `use` attribute set to `literal`, support for cyclic references and arrays is effectively disabled.

The rest of this chapter uses examples to show how native representations are mapped to and from XML, starting with primitives and ending with custom serializers.

Primitives

Most of the popular SOAP containers provide built-in support for all of the standard Java data types and some common utility classes, mapping them onto the XSD data types as shown in Table 4.1.

TABLE 4.1
Java data types mapped to XSD

Java type	XSD type
boolean	boolean
byte	byte
char	unsignedShort
short	short
int	int
long	long
float	float
double	double
String	string
Date	dateTime
BigDecimal	Decimal

The following example illustrates a few of these data types being echoed between a client and a server. The `IPrimitive` interface defines methods that echo back their primitive arguments.

wsbook\src\book\mapping\IPrimitive.java

```java
package book.mapping;

import java.util.Date;

public interface IPrimitive
    {
    int echoInt( int value );
    String echoString( String value );
    Date echoDate( Date date );
    }
```

The Primitive class is an implementation of `IPrimitive`, and simply echoes back the values that it receives.

wsbook\src\book\mapping\server\Primitive.java

```
package book.mapping.server;

import java.util.Date;
import book.mapping.IPrimitive;

public class Primitive implements IPrimitive
  {
  public int echoInt( int value )
    {
    return value;
    }

  public String echoString( String value )
    {
    return value;
    }

  public Date echoDate( Date date )
    {
    return date;
    }
  }
```

The server hosts an instance of Primitive at http://localhost:8004/soap/
primitive.

wsbook\src\book\mapping\server\PrimitiveServer.java

```
package book.mapping.server;

import electric.server.http.HTTP;
import electric.registry.Registry;

public class PrimitiveServer
  {
  public static void main( String[] args ) throws Exception
    {
    HTTP.startup( "http://localhost:8004/soap" );
    Registry.publish( "primitive", new Primitive() );
    }
  }
```

The client sends an int, a String, and a Date to the server and displays the
values that are echoed back.

wsbook\src\book\mapping\client\PrimitiveClient.java

```
package book.mapping.client;

import java.util.Date;
import electric.registry.Registry;
import book.mapping.IPrimitive;

public class PrimitiveClient
  {
  public static void main( String[] args ) throws Exception
    {
    String url = "http://localhost:8004/soap/primitive.wsdl";
    IPrimitive echo = (IPrimitive) Registry.bind( url, IPrimitive.class );

    Date now = new Date();
    System.out.println( "echoInt( 42 ) = " + echo.echoInt( 42 ) );
    System.out.println( "echoString( \"cat\" ) = " + echo.echoString(
"cat" ) );
    System.out.println( "echoDate( " + now + " ) = " + echo.echoDate(
now ) );
    }
  }
```

To run the example, execute PrimitiveServer in one window and Primitive-Client in another. Here's the server output:

```
> java book.mapping.server.PrimitiveServer
GLUE 1.2 (c) 2001 The Mind Electric
startup server on http://199.174.17.11:8004/soap
```

Here's the client output:

```
> java book.mapping.client.PrimitiveClient
echoInt( 42 ) = 42
echoString( "cat" ) = cat
echoDate( Tue Aug 07 19:03:52 CDT 2001 ) = Tue Aug 07 19:03:52 CDT
2001
> _
```

Here is the SOAP body of the request that sends an int. The xsi:type attribute indicates that the element is an XSD int.

```
<soap:Body>
  <n:echoIntResponse
    xmlns:n='http://tempuri.org/book.mapping.server.Primitive'>
    <Result xsi:type='xsd:int'>42</Result>
  </n:echoIntResponse>
</soap:Body>
```

Here is the SOAP body of the request that sends a String. The xsi:type attribute indicates that the element is an XSD string.

```
<soap:Body>
  <n:echoString
    xmlns:n='http://tempuri.org/book.mapping.server.Primitive'>
    <value xsi:type='xsd:string'>cat</value>
  </n:echoString>
</soap:Body>
```

Here is the SOAP body of the request that sends a Date. The xsl:type attribute indicates that the element is an XSD date. The href, id, and root attributes are related to support for object graphs, discussed later in this chapter.

```
<soap:Body>
  <n:echoDate xmlns:n='http://tempuri.org/book.mapping.server.Primitive'>
    <date href='#id0'/>
  </n:echoDate>
  <id0 id='id0'
    soapenc:root='0' xsi:type='xsd:dateTime'>2001-08-08T04:29:40Z
  </id0>
</soap:Body>
```

Arrays

SOAP provides built-in support for encoding arrays, as well as a special format for efficiently encoding byte arrays. It also defines an encoding for sparse arrays that allows you to leave out elements that are equal to null.

The following example illustrates the transmission of a regular array and a byte array. The IArray interface defines methods that echo back an array of ints and an array of bytes.

wsbook\src\book\mapping\IArray.java

```
package book.mapping;

public interface IArray
  {
  int[] echoInts( int[] value );
  byte[] echoBytes( byte[] value );
  }
```

The ArrayServer class (not shown here because it's pretty trivial) hosts an implementation of `IArray` at http://localhost:8004/soap/array, and ArrayClient displays the result of sending an array of ints and bytes.

wsbook\src\book\mapping\client\ArrayClient.java

```
package book.mapping.client;

import electric.registry.Registry;
import book.mapping.IArray;

public class ArrayClient
  {
  public static void main( String[] args ) throws Exception
    {
    String url = "http://localhost:8004/soap/array.wsdl";
    IArray echo = (IArray) Registry.bind( url, IArray.class );

    int[] ints = echo.echoInts( new int[]{ 1, 2, 3 } );
    System.out.print( "echoInts( [1, 2, 3] ) => " );
    for( int i = 0; i < ints.length; i++ )
      System.out.print( ints[ i ] + " " );
    System.out.println();

    byte[] bytes = echo.echoBytes( new byte[]{ 1, 2, 3 } );
    System.out.print( "echoBytes( [1, 2, 3] ) => " );
    for( int i = 0; i < bytes.length; i++ )
      System.out.print( bytes[ i ] + " " );
    System.out.println();
    }
  }
```

To run the example, execute ArrayServer in one window and ArrayClient in another. Here's the server output:

```
> java book.mapping.server.ArrayServer
GLUE 1.2 (c) 2001 The Mind Electric
startup server on http://199.174.17.11:8004/soap
```

Here's the client output:

```
> java book.mapping.client.ArrayClient
echoInts( [1, 2, 3] ) => 1 2 3
echoBytes( [1, 2, 3] ) => 1 2 3
> _
```

Here is the SOAP body of the request that echos an array of ints. The xsi:type attribute indicates that the argument is a SOAP array, and the soapenc:arrayType attribute value indicates that the type of each element is an xsd:int. Each individual element is encoded separately, and may be assigned an arbitrary name. The href, id, and root attributes are related to object graphs, discussed later in this chapter.

```
<soap:Body>
  <n:echoInts xmlns:n='http://tempuri.org/book.mapping.server.Array'>
    <ints href='#id0'/>
  </n:echoInts>
  <id0 id='id0'
    soapenc:root='0'
    xsi:type='soapenc:Array'
    soapenc:arrayType='xsd:int[3]'>
    <i xsi:type='xsd:int'>1</i>
    <i xsi:type='xsd:int'>2</i>
    <i xsi:type='xsd:int'>3</i>
  </id0>
</soap:Body>
```

Here is the SOAP body of the request that echos an array of bytes. SOAP uses a special format called base 64 encoding for transmitting byte arrays, which convert the bytes into a sequence of ASCII characters. In this case, the three bytes are converted into the character sequence AQID.

```
<soap:Body>
  <n:echoBytes xmlns:n='http://tempuri.org/book.mapping.server.Array'>
    <bytes href='#id0'/>
  </n:echoBytes>
  <id0 id='id0' soapenc:root='0' xsi:type='xsd:base64Binary'>AQID</id0>
</soap:Body>
```

User-Defined Types

For a program to send and receive user-defined data types using SOAP, there must be a bidirectional mapping between its representation in the native programming language and an XML schema. This mapping can then be used to guide the encoding and decoding process.

In many cases, a straightforward default mapping can be created automatically by introspecting the native representation of the object.

The following example shows how a Quote object can easily be sent between two SOAP programs, and assumes that both the client and the server are using the same native representation. Later on in this chapter, I'll show you how to send objects between systems without making this assumption.

The following IUser interface defines a method that echoes its Quote input.

wsbook\src\book\mapping\IUser.java

```
package book.mapping;

public interface IUser
  {
  Quote echoQuote( Quote quote );
  }
```

The Quote class, which is used by both the client and the server, defines two primitive fields and some accessors that follow the JavaBeans naming convention.

wsbook\src\book\mapping\Quote.java

```
package book.mapping;

public class Quote
  {
  String symbol;
  float price;

  public Quote()
    {
    }

  public Quote( String symbol, float price )
    {
    this.symbol = symbol;
    this.price = price;
    }

  public String toString()
    {
    return "Quote( " + symbol + ", " + price + " )";
    }

  public String getSymbol()
    {
    return symbol;
    }
```

```
  public void setSymbol( String symbol )
    {
    this.symbol = symbol;
    }

  public float getPrice()
    {
    return price;
    }

  public void setPrice( float price )
    {
    this.price = price;
    }
  }
```

The server publishes an implementation of IUser at http://localhost:8004/ soap/user that simply echoes values that are sent to it.

wsbook\src\book\mapping\server\UserServer.java

```
package book.mapping.server;

import electric.server.http.HTTP;
import electric.registry.Registry;

public class UserServer
  {
  public static void main( String[] args ) throws Exception
    {
    HTTP.startup( "http://localhost:8004/soap" );
    Registry.publish( "user", new User() );
    }
  }
```

If you type http://localhost:8004/soap/user.wsdl into a browser, you'll see the WSDL for the user service, which includes the following <types> section:

```
<types>
  <schema xmlns='http://www.w3.org/2001/XMLSchema'
    xmlns:tns='http://www.themindelectric.com/package/book.mapping/'
    targetNamespace='http://www.themindelectric.com/package/
book.mapping/'>
    <complexType name='Quote'>
      <sequence>
        <element name='symbol' type='string'/>
        <element name='price' type='float'/>
      </sequence>
    </complexType>
  </schema>
</types>
```

By default, GLUE creates a complex type for each class of argument, placing the class with name a.b.C to an XML complexType called C in the namespace http://www.themindelectric.com/package/a.b.. It uses reflection to determine the fields of each class, and maps them onto similarly named elements in a sequence. Several other SOAP platforms take a similar approach. Later in this chapter I'll show how these default rules can be overridden.

The client creates an instance of Quote and displays the value that is echoed from the server.

wsbook\src\book\mapping\client\UserClient.java

```
package book.mapping.client;

import electric.registry.Registry;
import book.mapping.IUser;
import book.mapping.Quote;

public class UserClient
   {
   public static void main( String[] args ) throws Exception
      {
      String url = "http://localhost:8004/soap/user.wsdl";
      IUser echo = (IUser) Registry.bind( url, IUser.class );

      Quote quote = new Quote( "IBM", 106.1F );
      System.out.println( "echoQuote(" + quote + ") = " +
echo.echoQuote( quote ) );
      }
   }
```

To run the example, execute UserServer in one window and UserClient in another. Here's the server output:

```
> java book.mapping.server.UserServer
GLUE 1.2 (c) 2001 The Mind Electric
startup server on http://199.174.17.11:8004/soap
```

Here's the client output:

```
> java book.mapping.client.UserClient
echoQuote( Quote( IBM, 106.1 ) ) = Quote( IBM, 106.1 )
> _
```

Here is the SOAP body of the request, which shows the XML encoding of the Quote object.

```
<soap:Body>
  <n:echoQuote xmlns:n='http://tempuri.org/book.mapping.server.User'>
    <quote href='#id0'/>
  </n:echoQuote>
  <id0 id='id0' soapenc:root='0'
   xmlns:ns2='http://www.themindelectric.com/package/book.mapping/'
    xsi:type='ns2:Quote'>
    <symbol xsi:type='xsd:string'>IBM</symbol>
    <price xsi:type='xsd:float'>106.1</price>
  </id0>
</soap:Body>
```

A null can be represented by an element with the attribute xsi:nil set to 1. For example, the trace for UserClient executed with a null quote looks like this:

```
<soap:Body>
  <n:echoQuote xmlns:n='http://tempuri.org/book.mapping.server.User'>
    <quote xsi:nil='1'/>
  </n:echoQuote>
</soap:Body>
```

Any Type

Many Java SOAP platforms map java.lang.Object to XSD anyType, which is compatible with any kind of XML data type. An Object parameter can therefore send and receive any kind of data. The receiver of the request uses the xsi:type attribute to figure out what type of argument has been sent.

The following example illustrates the transmission of two different data types via an anyType argument. The IAny interface defines a method that echoes back its input parameter.

wsbook\src\book\mapping\IAny.java

```
package book.mapping;

public interface IAny
  {
  Object echo( Object object );
  }
```

The AnyServer (not shown) program hosts an implementation of IAny at http://localhost:8004/soap/any that echoes back values that are sent to it, and the AnyClient program displays the result of echoing a String and a Quote.

wsbook\src\book\mapping\client\AnyClient.java

```
package book.mapping.client;

import electric.registry.Registry;
import book.mapping.IAny;
import book.mapping.Quote;

public class AnyClient
   {
   public static void main( String[] args ) throws Exception
      {
      String url = "http://localhost:8004/soap/any.wsdl";
      IAny echo = (IAny) Registry.bind( url, IAny.class );

      Quote quote = new Quote( "IBM", 80.2F );
      System.out.println( "echo( \"cat\" ) = " + echo.echo( "cat" ) );
      System.out.println( "echo( " + quote + " ) = " + echo.echo( quote
) );
      }
   }
```

To run the example, execute AnyServer in one window and AnyClient in another. Here's the server output:

```
> java book.mapping.server.AnyServer
GLUE 1.2 (c) 2001 The Mind Electric
startup server on http://199.174.17.11:8004/soap
```

Here's the client output:

```
> java book.mapping.client.AnyClient
echo( "cat" ) = cat
echo( Quote( IBM, 80.2 ) ) = Quote( IBM, 80.2 )
> _
```

If you look at the WSDL at http://localhost:8004/soap/any.wsdl, you can see that the argument and return type for the echo operation are both set to anyType:

```
http://localhost:8004/soap/any.wsdl

<definitions>
  ...
  <message name='echo0SoapIn'>
    <part name='value' type='xsd:anyType'/>
  </message>

  <message name='echo0SoapOut'>
    <part name='Result' type='xsd:anyType'/>
  </message>

  <portType name=book.mapping.server.AnySoap'>
    <operation name='echo' parameterOrder='value'>
      <input name='echo0SoapIn' message='tns:echo0SoapIn'/>
      <output name='echo0SoapOut' message='tns:echo0SoapOut'/>
    </operation>
  </portType>
  ...
</definitions>
```

Object Graphs

The standard SOAP encoding scheme allows object graphs to be serialized and deserialized in a manner that preserves morphology. For example, if *A* and *B* both point to a single *C* object before serialization, then after deserialization, *A* and *B* will still both point to a single *C* object rather than pointing to separate copies of *C* (see Figure 4.3).

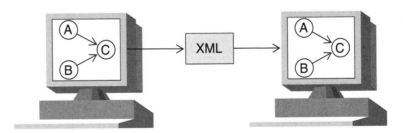

FIGURE 4.3
SOAP encoding preserves morphology

The following example illustrates this by echoing two arrays of Quote objects. One contains two references to different Quote objects, and the other contains two references to the same Quote object. When the arrays are echoed, the references are compared using == to see if they point to the same object.

wsbook\src\book\mapping\client\GraphClient.java

```
package book.mapping.client;

import electric.registry.Registry;
import book.mapping.IAny;
import book.mapping.Quote;

public class GraphClient
  {
  public static void main( String[] args ) throws Exception
    {
    String url = "http://localhost:8004/soap/any.wsdl";
    IAny echo = (IAny) Registry.bind( url, IAny.class );

    Quote quote1 = new Quote( "IBM", 106.1F );
    Quote quote2 = new Quote( "IBM", 106.1F );

    Quote[] quotesA = new Quote[]{ quote1, quote2 };
    Quote[] quotesB = (Quote[]) echo.echo( quotesA );
    print( quotesA, quotesB );

    Quote[] quotesC = new Quote[]{ quote1, quote1 };
    Quote[] quotesD = (Quote[]) echo.echo( quotesC );
    print( quotesC, quotesD );
    }

  static void print( Quote[] quotes1, Quote[] quotes2 )
    {
    System.out.println( "sent: " + quotes1[ 0 ] + ", " + quotes1[ 1 ]
);
    System.out.println( "received: " + quotes2[ 0 ] + ", " + quotes2[
1 ] );
    System.out.println( "identical: " + (quotes2[ 0 ] == quotes2[ 1
]) );
    System.out.println();
    }
  }
```

To run the example, execute AnyServer in one window and GraphClient in another. Here's the client output. As expected, only the second value that was echoed contains two references to the same Quote object.

```
> java book.mapping.client.GraphClient
sent: Quote( IBM, 106.1 ), Quote( IBM, 106.1 )
received: Quote( IBM, 106.1 ), Quote( IBM, 106.1 )
identical: false

sent: Quote( IBM, 106.1 ), Quote( IBM, 106.1 )
received: Quote( IBM, 106.1 ), Quote( IBM, 106.1 )
identical: true
> _
```

SOAP supports serialization of object graphs by requiring all nonprimitive elements to be assigned a unique id and stored in a separate element following the message payload. Each nonprimitive argument refers to its corresponding element by supplying an href attribute with the id. The soapenc:root attribute denotes the top level of serialization for each value.

In the first request, the array elements referred to separate Quote objects, so the encoded array uses href to access the separate elements with identifiers id1 and id2. The id and href attributes are bolded for clarity.

```
<soap:Body>
  <n:echo xmlns:n='http://tempuri.org/book.mapping.server.Any'>
    <value href='#id0'/>
  </n:echo>
  <id0 id='id0' soapenc:root='0'
    xmlns:ns2='http://www.themindelectric.com/package/book.mapping/'
    xsi:type='soapenc:Array' soapenc:arrayType='ns2:Quote[2]'>
    <i href='#id1'/>
    <i href='#id2'/>
  </id0>
  <id1 id='id1' soapenc:root='0'
    xmlns:ns2='http://www.themindelectric.com/package/book.mapping/'
    xsi:type='ns2:Quote'>
    <symbol xsi:type='xsd:string'>IBM</symbol>
    <price xsi:type='xsd:float'>106.1</price>
  </id1>
  <id2 id='id2' soapenc:root='0'
    xmlns:ns2='http://www.themindelectric.com/package/book.mapping/'
    xsi:type='ns2:Quote'>
    <symbol xsi:type='xsd:string'>IBM</symbol>
    <price xsi:type='xsd:float'>106.1</price>
  </id2>
</soap:Body>
```

In the second request, the array elements referred to the same Quote object, so the encoded array uses href to access the shared value with identifier id1.

```
<soap:Body>
  <n:echo xmlns:n='http://tempuri.org/book.mapping.server.Any'>
    <value href='#id0'/>
  </n:echo>
  <id0 id='id0' soapenc:root='0'
    xmlns:ns2='http://www.themindelectric.com/package/book.mapping/'
    xsi:type='soapenc:Array' soapenc:arrayType='ns2:Quote[2]'>
    <i href='#id1'/>
    <i href='#id1'/>
  </id0>
  <id1 id='id1' soapenc:root='0'
    xmlns:ns2='http://www.themindelectric.com/package/book.mapping/'
    xsi:type='ns2:Quote'>
    <symbol xsi:type='xsd:string'>IBM</symbol>
    <price xsi:type='xsd:float'>106.1</price>
  </id1>
</soap:Body>
```

User-Defined Mappings

As I mentioned earlier in this chapter, many SOAP platforms will map a class to an XML schema by associating each field of the class with an element of a sequence. This section addresses two questions:

- How can a SOAP server override the default mapping rules?
- How can a client generate the data structures necessary to communicate with a SOAP server?

I'll answer these questions using a simple example in which a client sends an invoice to an accounting service and receives a receipt. The mechanism for performing native/XML mapping varies from platform to platform, so this section describes the GLUE approach.

The Invoice class defines a field for the invoice number, a field for the invoice amount, a couple of constructors, and accessors named according to the JavaBean naming convention.

wsbook\src\book\mapping\server\Invoice.java

```
package book.mapping.server;

public class Invoice
  {
  int number;
  float amount;

  public Invoice()
```

```
    {
    }
  public Invoice( int number, float amount )
    {
    this.number = number;
    this.amount = amount;
    }

  public String toString()
    {
    return "Invoice( " + number + ", " + amount + " )";
    }

  public int getNumber()
    {
    return number;
    }

  public void setNumber( int number )
    {
    this.number = number;
    }

  public float getAmount()
    {
    return amount;
    }

  public void setAmount( float amount )
    {
    this.amount = amount;
    }
  }
```

The Receipt class defines a field for a copy of the invoice, a field for the date the invoice was paid, a couple of constructors, and accessors named according to the JavaBean naming convention.

wsbook\src\book\mapping\server\Receipt.java

```
package book.mapping.server;

import java.util.Date;

public class Receipt
  {
  Invoice invoice;
  Date paid;

  public Receipt()
    {
```

```
      }
   public Receipt( Invoice invoice, Date paid )
      {
      this.invoice = invoice;
      this.paid = paid;
      }

   public String toString()
      {
      return "Receipt( " + invoice + ", " + paid + " )";
      }

   public Invoice getInvoice()
      {
      return invoice;
      }

   public void setInvoice( Invoice invoice )
      {
      this.invoice = invoice;
      }

   public Date getPaid()
      {
      return paid;
      }

   public void setPaid( Date paid )
      {
      this.paid = paid;
      }
   }
```

The Accounting class accepts an invoice and returns a receipt with the paid field set to the current date.

wsbook\src\book\mapping\server\Accounting.java

```
package book.mapping.server;

import java.util.Date;

public class Accounting
   {
   public Receipt invoice( Invoice invoice )
      {
      Date paid = new Date();
      return new Receipt( invoice, paid );
      }
   }
```

By default, each field of the Receipt and Invoice classes are mapped to a corresponding element in an XML Schema. To map the paid field of a receipt to an XML attribute instead of an element, first use the java2schema utility to create a .map file that describes the default mapping. Type the following command from the wsbook\src\book\mapping\server directory.

```
> java2schema book.mapping.server.Receipt
write file Receipt.map
> _
```

A .map file contains annotated XML schemas that indicate class mappings. Here is what the default Receipt.map file looks like, with annotations bolded for clarity.

wsbook\src\book\mapping\server\Receipt.map (before modification)

```
<?xml version='1.0' encoding='UTF-8'?>
<mappings xmlns='http://www.themindelectric.com/schema/'>
  <schema xmlns='http://www.w3.org/2001/XMLSchema'
targetNamespace='http://www.themindelectric.com/package/
book.mapping.server/' xmlns:electric='http://www.themindelectric.com/
schema/'>
    <complexType name='Receipt'
electric:class='book.mapping.server.Receipt'>
      <sequence>
        <element name='invoice' nillable='true'
electric:field='invoice' xmlns:ns3='http://www.themindelectric.com/
package/book.mapping.server/' type='ns3:Invoice'/>
        <element name='paid' nillable='true' electric:field='paid'
type='dateTime'/>
      </sequence>
    </complexType>
  </schema>
</mappings>
```

There are five annotation attributes:

electric:class='qualified-java-class-name'	This Java class that the annotated schema type maps to.
electric:property='name-of-javabean-property'	The JavaBean property that should be used when reading/writing the annotated element/attribute.

electric:field='name-of-field'	The Java field that should be used when reading/writing the annotated element/attribute.
electric:get='name-of-get-accessor'	The accessor that should be used when reading the annotated element/attribute.
electric:set='name-of-set-accessor'	The accessor that should be used when writing the annotated element/attribute.

In this case, the Receipt.map file indicates that the XML schema type with namespace http://www.themindelectric.com/package/book.mapping.server and name Receipt is mapped to the Java class called book.mapping.server.Receipt, the invoice element is mapped to the Java field called invoice, and the paid element is mapped to the Java field called paid.

To map the Java field called paid to an attribute instead, edit Receipt.map to look like the following file. The changed line is bolded for clarity.

wsbook\src\book\mapping\server\Receipt.map (after edit)

```
<?xml version='1.0' encoding='UTF-8'?>
<mappings xmlns='http://www.themindelectric.com/schema/'>
  <schema xmlns='http://www.w3.org/2001/XMLSchema'
targetNamespace='http://www.themindelectric.com/package/
book.mapping.server/' xmlns:electric='http://www.themindelectric.com/
schema/'>
    <complexType name='Receipt'
electric:class='book.mapping.server.Receipt'>
      <sequence>
        <element name='invoice' nillable='true'
electric:field='invoice' xmlns:ns3='http://www.themindelectric.com/
package/book.mapping.server/' type='ns3:Invoice'/>
      </sequence>
      <attribute name='paid' nillable='true' electric:field='paid'
type='dateTime'/>
    </complexType>
  </schema>
</mappings>
```

Map files must be explicitly loaded at the start of a program to ensure that the default mappings are overridden. The AccountingServer program reads the mappings and publishes an Account service at http://localhost:8004/soap.

wsbook\src\book\mapping\server\AccountingServer.java

```
package book.mapping.server;

import electric.server.http.HTTP;
import electric.registry.Registry;
import electric.xml.io.Mappings;

public class AccountingServer
  {
  public static void main( String[] args ) throws Exception
    {
    Mappings.readMappings( "Receipt.map" );
    HTTP.startup( "http://localhost:8004/soap" );
    Registry.publish( "accounting", new Accounting() );
    }
  }
```

To run the server, execute AccountingServer from the wsbook\src\book\mapping\server directory. Here is the server output:

```
> java book.mapping.server.AccountingServer
GLUE 1.2 (c) 2001 The Mind Electric
startup server on http://199.174.55.151:8004/soap
```

When the server is running, open your browser on http://localhost:8004/soap/accounting.wsdl and you will see that the definition of Receipt uses an attribute to contain the paid value.

http://localhost:8004/soap/accounting.wsdl (snippet)

```
<schema xmlns='http://www.w3.org/2001/XMLSchema'
  xmlns:tns='http://www.themindelectric.com/package/
book.mapping.server/'
targetNamespace='http://www.themindelectric.com/package/
book.mapping.server/'>
  <complexType name='Receipt'>
    <sequence>
      <element name='invoice' type='tns:Invoice'/>
    </sequence>
    <attribute name='paid' type='dateTime'/>
  </complexType>
  <complexType name='Invoice'>
    <sequence>
      <element name='number' type='int'/>
      <element name='amount' type='float'/>
    </sequence>
  </complexType>
</schema>
```

Now that the server is running, it's time to focus on the client side. To generate a Java interface that declares the web service operations and Java classes that correspond to its XML schema types, use the wsdl2java utility. You can use the –p option to specify the package for the output classes. The utility also generates a single .map file that contains the default mappings related to that particular web service.

In this example, type the following command from the wsbook\src\book\mapping\client directory.

```
> wsdl2java http://localhost:8004/soap/accounting.wsdl -p
book.mapping.client
write file IAccounting.java
write file AccountingHelper.java
write file Receipt.java
write file Invoice.java
write file Accounting.map
> _
```

Here is the Invoice.java file that was automatically generated. By default, each element in the Invoice schema is mapped to a public field in the Invoice class.

wsbook\src\book\mapping\client\Invoice.java

```
// generated by GLUE
package book.mapping.client;

public class Invoice
   {
   public int number;
   public float amount;
   }
```

Here is the Receipt.java file that was automatically generated. By default, each element and attribute in the Receipt schema is mapped to a public field in the Receipt class.

wsbook\src\book\mapping\client\Receipt.java

```
// generated by GLUE
package book.mapping.client;

public class Receipt
   {
   public book.mapping.client.Invoice invoice;
```

```
public java.util.Date paid;
}
```

Here is the IAccounting.java file that was automatically generated which declares all of the operations that may be invoked on the web service.

wsbook\src\book\mapping\client\IAccounting.java

```
// generated by GLUE
package book.mapping.client;

public interface IAccounting
  {
  Receipt invoice( Invoice invoice );
  }
```

The Accounting.map file contains annotated schemas for the Invoice and Recipt data types based on the XML schema definitions. Annotations are shown in bold for clarity.

wsbook\src\book\mapping\client\Accounting.map

```
<?xml version='1.0' encoding='UTF-8'?>
<!--generated by GLUE-->
<mappings xmlns='http://www.themindelectric.com/schema/'>
  <schema xmlns='http://www.w3.org/2001/XMLSchema'
targetNamespace='http://www.themindelectric.com/package/
book.mapping.server/' xmlns:electric='http://www.themindelectric.com/
schema/'>
    <complexType name='Receipt'
electric:class='book.mapping.client.Receipt'>
      <sequence>
        <element name='invoice' nillable='true'
electric:field='invoice' xmlns:ns3='http://www.themindelectric.com/
package/book.mapping.server/' type='ns3:Invoice'/>
      </sequence>
      <attribute name='paid' electric:field='paid' type='dateTime'/>
    </complexType>
  </schema>
  <schema xmlns='http://www.w3.org/2001/XMLSchema'
targetNamespace='http://www.themindelectric.com/package/
book.mapping.server/' xmlns:electric='http://www.themindelectric.com/
schema/'>
    <complexType name='Invoice'
electric:class='book.mapping.client.Invoice'>
      <sequence>
```

```
            <element name='number' electric:field='number' type='int'/>
            <element name='amount' electric:field='amount' type='float'/>
        </sequence>
      </complexType>
    </schema>
</mappings>
```

This file can be modified if you wish to change the client-side mappings.

The AccountClient program reads the client-side mapping file and invokes the remote web service. Note that no custom serialization code was necessary on the client or the server in order to map Java to and from XML.

wsbook\src\book\mapping\client\AccountingClient.java

```
package book.mapping.client;

import electric.registry.Registry;
import electric.xml.io.Mappings;

public class AccountingClient
  {
  public static void main( String[] args ) throws Exception
    {
    Mappings.readMappings( "Accounting.map" );
    IAccounting accounting = AccountingHelper.bind();

    Invoice invoice = new Invoice();
    invoice.number = 918;
    invoice.amount = 19.62F;

    Receipt receipt = accounting.invoice( invoice );

    System.out.println( "receipt.paid = " + receipt.paid );
    System.out.println( "receipt.invoice.number = " +
receipt.invoice.number );
    System.out.println( "receipt.invoice.amount = " +
receipt.invoice.amount );
    }
  }
```

To run the example, make sure the AccountingServer is running, and then run AccountingClient from the wsbook\src\book\mapping\client directory. Here's the client output:

```
> java book.mapping.client.AccountingClient
receipt.paid = Tue Aug 07 20:05:10 CDT 2001
receipt.invoice.number = 918
receipt.invoice.amount = 19.62
> _
```

Here is the SOAP body of the request, which shows the XML encoding of the Invoice object.

```
<soap:Body>
  <n:invoice xmlns:n='http://tempuri.org/book.mapping.server.Accounting'>
    <invoice href='#id0'/>
  </n:invoice>
  <id0 id='id0' soapenc:root='0'
   xmlns:ns2='http://www.themindelectric.com/package/book.mapping.server/'
    xsi:type='ns2:Invoice'>
    <number xsi:type='xsd:int'>918</number>
    <amount xsi:type='xsd:float'>19.62</amount>
  </id0>
</soap:Body>
```

Here is the SOAP body of the response, which shows the XML encoding of the Receipt object that contains the original Invoice. Note that the paid field is encoded as an attribute, not an element, due to the settings in the Receipt.map file.

```
<soap:Body>
  <n:invoiceResponse
    xmlns:n='http://tempuri.org/book.mapping.server.Accounting'>
    <Result href='#id0'/>
  </n:invoiceResponse>
  <id0 id='id0' soapenc:root='0'
    xmlns:ns2='http://www.themindelectric.com/package/
book.mapping.server/'
    xsi:type='ns2:Receipt' paid='Fri Sep 28 13:44:15 CDT 2001'>
    <invoice href='#id1'/>
  </id0>
  <id1 id='id1' soapenc:root='0'
    xmlns:ns2='http://www.themindelectric.com/package/
book.mapping.server/'
    xsi:type='ns2:Invoice'>
    <number xsi:type='xsd:int'>918</number>
    <amount xsi:type='xsd:float'>19.62</amount>
  </id1>
</soap:Body>
```

Custom Types

Although most SOAP platforms include a high-level mechanism for describing the native/XML mapping process, there are times when you need to write code to obtain complete low-level control over a particular mapping.

For example, if you want to map a Java Hashtable to XML, there is no straightforward mapping between its fields and an XML respresentation, so custom code is needed. Each SOAP platform has its own API for creating a custom mapping. GLUE requires you to create a subclass of Type that overrides the following methods:

writeSchema(Element schema)	This method writes an XML Schema definition to the incoming schema Element. To obtain the qualified name of a Java class relative to a particular element, use `getName( Element element, Class javaClass )`.
writeObject(IWriter writer, Object object)	This method writes the object to the writer. Before writing the contents of the object, you should call `writer.writeType( this )`, which writes the `xsi:type` attribute.
readObject(IReader reader, Value value)	This method reads the object from the reader and calls `value.setObject()` with the reconstructed object. GLUE can handle cyclic references to an object once `setObject()` has been called, so ideally you should create the object and call `setObject()` before reconstructing its state.
addDependencies(Vector dependencies)	This method must add any additional Types that this class references, and is used by the WSDL generator to compute the closure of the web service. Use `Type.getType( Class javaClass )` to obtain the Type associated with a particular Java class.

The custom Type object can then be registered to perform mappings between the Java class and XML schema type defined by `writeSchema()`.

Complete information on how to write custom types are beyond the scope of this book, and vary enough between SOAP platforms that it's best to refer to the platform user guide for the details. The following examples are intended to give you a feel for what is generally involved.

Here is the built-in custom type which GLUE uses to map Hashtables to XML.

```
package electric.xml.io.collections1;

import java.io.*;
import java.util.*;
import electric.xml.*;
import electric.xml.io.*;
import electric.util.Value;
```

```
public class HashtableType extends Type
  {
  public void writeSchema( Element schema )
    {
    Element complexType = schema.addElement( "complexType" );
    complexType.setAttribute( "name", "Map" );
    Element sequence = complexType.addElement( "sequence" );
    Element element = sequence.addElement( "element" );
    element.setAttribute( "name", "item" );
    element.setAttribute( "minOccurs", "0" );
    element.setAttribute( "maxOccurs", "unbounded" );
    Element subType = element.addElement( "complexType" );
    Element subSequence = subType.addElement( "sequence" );
    Element key = subSequence.addElement( "element" );
    key.setAttribute( "name", "key" );
    key.setAttribute( "type", getName( key, Object.class ) );
    Element value = subSequence.addElement( "element" );
    value.setAttribute( "name", "value" );
    value.setAttribute( "type", getName( key, Object.class ) );
    }

  public void writeObject( IWriter writer, Object object )
    throws IOException
    {
    writer.writeType( this );
    Hashtable hashtable = (Hashtable) object;

    for( Enumeration enum = hashtable.keys(); enum.hasMoreElements(); )
      {
      Object key = enum.nextElement();
      Object value = hashtable.get( key );
      IWriter itemWriter = writer.writeElement( "item" );
      itemWriter.writeObject( "key", key );
      itemWriter.writeObject( "value", value );
      }
    }

  public void readObject( IReader reader, Value value )
    throws IOException
    {
    Hashtable hashtable = new Hashtable();
    value.setObject( hashtable );
    IReader[] readers = reader.getReaders( "item" );

    for( int i = 0; i < readers.length; i++ )
      {
      IReader itemReader = readers[ i ];
      Object key = itemReader.readObject( "key" );
      Object theValue = itemReader.readObject( "value" );
      hashtable.put( key, theValue );
      }
    }
  }
```

The following example shows this custom type in action. The CustomClient program displays the result of echoing a Hashtable to the AnyServer program that appeared earlier in this chapter.

wsbook\src\book\mapping\client\CustomClient.java

```
package book.mapping.client;

import java.util.Hashtable;
import electric.registry.Registry;
import book.mapping.IAny;

public class CustomClient
  {
  public static void main( String[] args ) throws Exception
    {
    String url = "http://localhost:8004/soap/any.wsdl";
    IAny echo = (IAny) Registry.bind( url, IAny.class );

    Hashtable table = new Hashtable();
    table.put( "AU", "gold" );
    table.put( "FE", "iron" );
    System.out.println( "echo( " + table + " ) = " + echo.echo( table ) );
    }
  }
```

To run the example, run AnyServer in one window and CustomClient in another. Here's the client output:

```
> java book.mapping.client.CustomClient
echo( {AU=gold, FE=iron} ) = {AU=gold, FE=iron}
> _
```

Here is the SOAP body of the request that sends the Hashtable. Note that the Hashtable is mapped to a sequence of items, as defined by the custom type.

```
<soap:Body>
  <n:echo xmlns:n='http://tempuri.org/book.mapping.server.Any'>
    <value href='#id0'/>
  </n:echo>
  <id0 id='id0' soapenc:root='0' xmlns:ns2='http://xml.apache.org/
xml-soap'
    xsi:type='ns2:Map'>
    <item>
      <key xsi:type='xsd:string'>AU</key>
      <value xsi:type='xsd:string'>gold</value>
    </item>
    <item>
```

```
      <key xsi:type='xsd:string'>FE</key>
      <value xsi:type='xsd:string'>iron</value>
    </item>
  </id0>
</soap:Body>
```

The next example performs the same custom mapping for Receipt that was achieved using annotated schemas earlier in this chapter. As you can tell from looking at the source code for ReceiptType.java, it's a good idea to use a platform's high-level mapping scheme whenever possible, because low-level mapping code can be quite intricate and error-prone.

wsbook\src\book\mapping\server\ReceiptType.java

```java
package book.mapping.server;

import java.io.IOException;
import java.util.*;
import electric.util.Value;
import electric.xml.*;
import electric.xml.io.*;

public class ReceiptType extends Type
  {
  public void addDependencies( Vector dependencies )
    {
    dependencies.addElement( getType( Invoice.class ) );
    }

  public void writeSchema( Element schema )
    {
    Element complexType = schema.addElement( "complexType" );
    complexType.setAttribute( "name", "Receipt" );
    Element sequence = complexType.addElement( "sequence" );
    Element invoice = sequence.addElement( "element" );
    invoice.setAttribute( "name", "invoice" );
    invoice.setAttribute( "type", getName( invoice, Invoice.class )
);
    Element paid = complexType.addElement( "attribute" );
    paid.setAttribute( "name", "paid" );
    paid.setAttribute( "type", getName( paid, Date.class ) );
    }

  public void writeObject( IWriter writer, Object object )
    throws IOException
    {
    Receipt receipt = (Receipt) object;
    writer.writeType( this );
    writer.writeAttribute( "paid", receipt.getPaid().toString() );
    writer.writeObject( "invoice", receipt.getInvoice() );
    }
```

```
 public void readObject( IReader reader, Value value )
    throws IOException
    {
    Receipt receipt = new Receipt();
    value.setObject( receipt );
    receipt.setPaid( new Date( reader.readAttributeValue( "paid" ) )
);
    receipt.setInvoice( (Invoice) reader.readObject( "invoice" ) );
    }
  }
```

The CustomServer program uses `Mappings.mapClass()` to specify the custom type to use when mapping between the Java class and its corresponding XML schema type.

wsbook\src\book\mapping\server\CustomServer.java

```
package book.mapping.server;

import electric.server.http.HTTP;
import electric.registry.Registry;
import electric.xml.io.Mappings;

public class CustomServer
  {
  public static void main( String[] args ) throws Exception
    {
    Mappings.mapClass( Receipt.class, "http://
www.themindelectric.com/package/book.mapping.server/", "Receipt",
ReceiptType.class );
    HTTP.startup( "http://localhost:8004/soap" );
    Registry.publish( "accounting", new Accounting() );
    }
  }
```

To run the example, run CustomServer in one window and AccountingClient in another. The output should be exactly the same as it was earlier in the chapter.

Summary

In this chapter, we studied the mechanisms that can be used to map complex data structures to XML, and saw that annotated schemas allow mappings to be defined without the need for custom code.

We also noted that each SOAP platform typically includes its own mapping system, and that there is no accepted standard for performing this task.

Quiz

- What is special about the XSD data type called anyType?
- How is a null value encoded?
- Why is support for graph encoding sometimes called `id/href` encoding?
- What does "section 5 encoding" mean?
- When would you use base64 encoding?
- What is an annotated schema?
- Under what situations do you need to write a custom serializer?

Exercises

1. Write a Java class that represents a linked list and then figure out how to sent it using SOAP.
2. Create a web service using another platform like Apache SOAP and then send it a Hashtable.
3. What kind of IDE integration could make XML mapping even simpler?

Security

5

If you wish to deploy a web service into an open environment like the Internet, it's likely that you'll want to secure it in some way. There are currently no security standards that are specific to web services, but the existing standards for secure and authenticated HTTP can be used in most cases.

This chapter covers three different but complementary ways to secure web services, two of them already commonly in use, and the third in experimental stages.

- *HTTPS*, which is HTTP running over SSL. HTTPS uses a digital certificate scheme that allows the client and server to verify each other's identity and communicate over a secure, encrypted channel. HTTPS is built into most web browsers and is used by most e-commerce applications that run over the web.

- *HTTP basic authentication*, which allows specific URLs to be password protected so that only clients with the appropriate credentials can gain access. The most common use of this is by for-fee web sites. When you pay your subscription, these sites send you a password by email for the protected area of the site. When you attempt to access a protected area, the web server returns a special error code to your browser, which then issues a prompt for your user and password. Once the information is entered, the browser resubmits the request with the user and password as part of the HTTP header. If the credentials are correct, the contents of the URL are returned. The browser remembers the credentials and resubmits them automatically for the duration of that session.

- *SOAP security extensions*, which allow individual pieces of a payload to be electronically signed and encypted.

Let's start with HTTPS.

HTTPS

HTTPS uses a certificate scheme to allow the client and server to verify each other's identity.

In the most common scenario, a company that wishes to run an SSL server purchases a digital certificate from an issuing authority such as VeriSign. Issuing authorities perform due diligence before issuing a certificate, and require various legal documents that verify your identity. Once issued, the certificate basically means, "a well-known issuing authority has verified my identity." Clients of the company do not typically purchase certificates, since the server generally doesn't care who the clients are. However, the client software checks that the server has the appropriate certificate before forming a secure channel to the server. This at least ensures that there's a chain of trust back to an issuing company, and a way to identify the server if the transaction goes awry.

SSL capabilities are built into all browsers and web servers, and are also available to applications via libraries such as Java Secure Socket Extensions (JSSE), which is now part of the Java standard distribution.

The tools and APIs for manipulating certificates and creating secure socket connections vary among vendors. In this section I'll show you how to use JSSE to create an SSL connection using the GLUE platform that ships with this book. The approach is very similar if you use IBM Web Services Toolkit or Microsoft .NET.

Please note that JSSE works only with JDK 1.2 and above. If you are using JDK 1.1, you won't be able to run the examples in this section.

The JDK includes a standard set of certificates stored in the lib/security/cacerts file under the home directory of your Java Runtime Environment (JRE). This certificate set is called your *trust store* and allows a Java client to access any SSL server that has a certificate from a well-known issuing authority.

JSSE includes a utility called keytool that allows you to create self-signed certificates for internal use so you don't have to purchase a VeriSign certificate in order to experiment with SSL applications. Before running the example SSL program, you must run keytool to create your own certificate.

The following example assumes that your JRE is located in \jdk1.3\jre, and uses the initial preset password of changeit. To run the example yourself, replace the example fields with ones that are appropriate to yourself. Note that the first two lines of text should be entered onto a single command line.

```
> keytool -genkey -alias test -keyalg rsa -keystore
  \jdk1.3\jre\lib\security\cacerts
Enter keystore password:  changeit
What is your first and last name?
  [Unknown]:  graham glass
What is the name of your organizational unit?
  [Unknown]:  development
What is the name of your organization?
  [Unknown]:  acme
What is the name of your City or Locality?
  [Unknown]:  dallas
What is the name of your State or Province?
  [Unknown]:  texas
What is the two-letter country code for this unit?
  [Unknown]:  tx
Is <CN=graham glass, OU=development, O=the mind electric, L=dallas,
ST=texas, C=tx> correct?
  [no]:  yes

Enter key password for <test>
  (RETURN if same as keystore password):

> _
```

At this point, your local trust store includes a new self-signed certificate that allows clients and servers to communicate using SSL as long as they both have access to the same trust store files. See the JSSE download documentation at http://java.sun.com/products/jsse for detailed information about keytool and other SSL utilities.

Programs that use JSSE must have the standard Java properties javax.net.ssl.trustStore and javax.net.ssl.trustStore-Password set to the location of the trust store and its password, respectively. The default settings work with a standard Java installation, and are equal to `<JRE.home>/lib/security/cacerts` and `changeit`.

The following example uses JSSE to start an HTTPS server that accepts incoming secure connection requests only. The only difference between this example and the previous examples involving an Exchange service is that the URLs start with https:// instead of http://.

Here is the source code for the SSL1 server that publishes an Exchange service on a secure port.

wsbook\src\book\security\SSL1.java

```
package book.security;

import electric.registry.Registry;
import electric.server.http.HTTP;
import book.soap.Exchange;

public class SSL1
  {
  public static void main( String[] args )
    throws Exception
    {
    // start a secure web server on port 8004, accept messages via /
soap
    HTTP.startup( "https://localhost:8004/soap" );

    // publish an instance of Exchange
    Exchange exchange = new Exchange();
    exchange.setValue( "usa", 1 );
    exchange.setValue( "japan", 0.4 );
    Registry.publish( "exchange", exchange );
    }
  }
```

Here is the client code that accesses the published service using an HTTPS connection. Note that the URL of the service WSDL starts with https:// instead of http:/.

wsbook\src\book\security\SSL2.java

```
package book.security;

import electric.registry.Registry;
import book.soap.IExchange;

public class SSL2
  {
```

```
   public static void main( String[] args )
     throws Exception
     {
     // bind to secure web service at specified URL
     String url = "https://localhost:8004/soap/exchange.wsdl";
     IExchange exchange = (IExchange) Registry.bind( url,
IExchange.class );

     // invoke the web service as if it was a local java object
     double rate = exchange.getRate( "usa", "japan" );
     System.out.println( "usa/japan exchange rate = " + rate );
     }
   }
```

When you run SSL1 followed by SSL2, the SSL authenticating handshakes take place automatically, and the information between the programs is automatically secure and encrypted.

Here is the output from the server.

```
> java book.security.SSL1
GLUE 1.2 (c) 2001 The Mind Electric
startup server on https://199.174.55.92:8004/soap
```

Here is the output from the client.

```
> java book.security.SSL2
usa/japan exchange rate = 2.5

> _
```

If you are using self-signed certificates and the client and server do not both have the certificate in their truststores, an exception is thrown which says that no trusted certificate chain exists.

As you can see, writing web services programs that use HTTPS is very easy.

HTTP Basic Authentication

HTTP basic authentication allows servers to prevent access to specific URLs unless the requestor can provide user/password credentials, and is usually used in conjunction with HTTPS as part of a security solution.

There are four terms that are commonly used when discussing HTTP authentication:

1. *Principal*, an entity such as an individual or corporation.

2. *Role*, a category that can apply to a set of principals.

3. *Permission*, an action that can be performed on a particular resource by a specific principal or role.

4. *Realm*, a collection of information about principals, roles, and permissions.

For example, if the principal "graham" has roles "developer" and "architect," and all principals with the "architect" role have the ability to POST to the URL for web service X, then "graham" could POST messages to web service X. Companies normally set up a realm that stores information about their principals, roles, and permissions, and allow applications to connect to the realm in order to perform authentication.

If a plain HTTP request is made to an authenticating resource, the web server rejects the request by returning status code 401 (unauthorized) together with a WWW-Authenticate header that includes the name of the realm that the web server is using for authentication. The client must then resend the request with an Authorization header that includes a user/password combination that authenticates the client for the specified realm. Most clients choose to proactively send authenticated HTTP requests to avoid this initial challenge-response round trip.

User/password information is sent as a base-64 encoded string to allow any combination of characters to be used. Assuming that the user/password is correct, the server determines the roles that the user has and makes sure that the resource can be accessed by one of those roles. Assuming that everything is okay, the request is granted. Clients usually remember which resources require authentication and proactively include the user/password header in all subsequent requests to that URL.

The following example uses HTTPS in conjunction with HTTP basic authentication to provide encrypted and authenticated access to a web service. To simplify matters, the server creates a local realm that contains the authentication information. In an intranet environment, there would normally be a single shared realm that is accessed by all servers on the intranet.

The following server first creates a realm called `myrealm` and a principal called `graham` with password `kitty` and role `developer`. It then starts up an HTTPS server on port 8004 and tells it to use "myrealm" for all authentication. Next, it publishes an Exchange web service with a Context object that includes a guard to limit access to principals with the developer role.

wsbook\src\book\security\Authentication1.java

```
package book.security;

import electric.registry.Registry;
import electric.server.http.HTTP;
import electric.net.http.HTTPContext;
import electric.security.*;
import electric.util.Context;
import book.soap.Exchange;

public class Authentication1
  {
  public static void main( String[] args )
    throws Exception
    {
    // construct local realm
    BasicRealm myRealm = new BasicRealm( "myrealm" );

    // add realm to collection of registered realms
    Realms.addRealm( myRealm );

    // add principal with name="graham", password="kitty",
role="developer"
    myRealm.addPrincipal( "graham", "kitty", new String[]{
"developer" } );

    // start secure web server on port 8004, accept messages via /
soap
    HTTPContext httpContext = HTTP.startup( "https://localhost:8004/
soap" );

    // set realm for this context
    httpContext.setRealm( myRealm );

    // publish an instance of Exchange with context that includes
guard
    Context context = new Context();
    context.addProperty( "guard", new HasRole( "developer" ) );
    Exchange exchange = new Exchange();
    exchange.setValue( "usa", 1 );
    exchange.setValue( "japan", 0.4 );
    Registry.publish( "exchange", exchange, context );
    }
  }
```

The client program uses a feature of GLUE that allows you to use a Context object to pass a set of properties to bind(). The properties "authUser" and "authPassword" are automatically used as credentials when the server requires authentication.

wsbook\src\book\security\Authentication2.java

```
package book.security;

import electric.registry.Registry;
import electric.security.*;
import electric.util.*;
import book.soap.IExchange;

public class Authentication2
   {
   public static void main( String[] args )
     throws Exception
     {
     // bind to secure, authenticating web service at specified URL
     String url = "https://localhost:8004/soap/exchange.wsdl";
     Context context = new Context();
     context.setProperty( "authUser", "graham" );
     context.setProperty( "authPassword", "kitty" );
     IExchange exchange = (IExchange) Registry.bind( url,
IExchange.class, context );

     // invoke the web service as if it was a local java object
     double rate = exchange.getRate( "usa", "japan" );
     System.out.println( "usa/japan exchange rate = " + rate );
     }
   }
```

To run the example, execute Authentication1 in one window and Authentication2 in another. Here is the server output.

```
> java book.security.Authentication1
GLUE 1.2(c) 2001 The Mind Electric
startup server on https://199.174.55.92:8004/soap
```

If you run the client with HTTP logging enabled, you can see the authentication mechanism in action. Here is the client output, with the full text of the WSDL and SOAP responses omitted for clarity.

```
> java -Delectric.logging="HTTP" book.security.Authentication2
LOG.HTTP: outbound request to ssl://199.174.55.92:8004
GET /soap/exchange.wsdl HTTP/1.1
Host: localhost:8004
Connection: Keep-Alive
Authorization: Basic Z3JhaGFtOmtpdHR5

LOG.HTTP: response from ssl://199.174.55.92:8004
HTTP/1.1 200 OK
Content-Type: text/xml
```

```
Server: GLUE/1.0
Content-Length: 9553

<?xml version='1.0' encoding='UTF-8'?>
// WSDL transfer

LOG.HTTP: outbound request to ssl://199.174.55.92:8004
POST /soap/exchange HTTP/1.1
Host: 199.174.55.92:8004
Content-Type: text/xml
User-Agent: GLUE/1.0
Connection: Keep-Alive
SOAPAction: "exchange#getRate"
Content-Length: 533
Authorization: Basic Z3JhaGFtOmtpdHR5

<?xml version='1.0' encoding='UTF-8'?>
// SOAP request

LOG.HTTP: response from ssl://199.174.55.92:8004
HTTP/1.1 200 OK
Date: Wed, 04 Jul 2001 23:04:04 GMT
Content-Type: text/xml
Server: GLUE/1.0
Content-Length: 497

<?xml version='1.0' encoding='UTF-8'?>
// SOAP response

usa/japan exchange rate = 2.5

> _
```

SOAP Security Extensions

HTTPS combined with basic authentication is a good solution for securing single-hop messages, but does not work well if you want to implement multihop messages where intermediate nodes need to access the contents of the message. This is because SSL encrypts the entire payload at the sender and only decrypts it at the final destination.

One solution to this problem is to allow fields of a SOAP message to be individually secured using a public key encryption method so that each node is able to access fields for which it has the private key. In addition, some fields can be left unsecured and thus visible to all nodes. For example, a client could send a purchase request with the item and quantity out in the open but with the credit card number encrypted.

Figure 5.1 illustrates the basic idea:

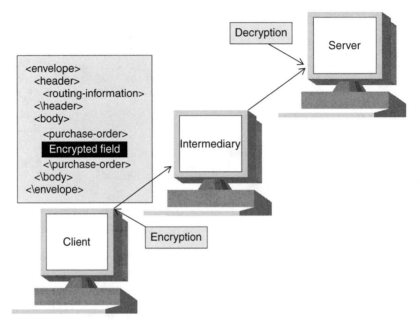

FIGURE 5.1
SOAP fields can be individually encrypted

Microsoft, IBM, and others are working on a standard to allow this approach to be used in a multivendor setting, and IBM has already released a prototype called SOAP Security Extensions that is part of its web services toolkit.

In the short term, most web services applications do not need field-level encryption, but in the long term, this capability will probably become quite popular.

Summary

In this chapter, we examined three different and complementary ways to secure SOAP messaging between web services.

We also used JSSE to run programs that used HTTPS and HTTP basic authentication.

In the next chapter, we'll look at UDDI, the web services matchmaker. Many UDDI servers use HTTPS as a means to secure important UDDI messages.

Quiz _____

- What does SSL stand for?
- What do the terms principal, role, permission, and realm mean?
- What is the problem with using SSL in multihop situations?

Exercises _____

1. Find out why HTTP basic authentication uses base-64 encoded strings.
2. Read the GLUE user guide and learn about how security works in the case of HTTP proxies.
3. Discuss the possible performance hits due to authentication and whether they are significant.

Universal Description, Discovery and Integration (UDDI)

UDDI allows information about a web service, such as its location, WSDL, and owner, to be published for use by other web services. It is the match-maker that enables the creation of fluid, dynamically assembled systems.

This chapter starts with a description of typical UDDI usage scenarios and outlines the difference between private and public UDDI registries. Then it provides an overview of the kinds of entities that are stored in a UDDI registry. The last two sections provide detailed examples of how to use the UDDI API to query and publish information about businesses and their services.

The examples use the GLUE UDDI API and the IBM UDDI registry, and can easily be modified to work with other UDDI clients and UDDI servers.

Scenarios

UDDI's main purpose is to provide an API for publishing and retrieving information about web services. Its operations can be invoked programmatically using a SOAP client or manually via a user interface.

UDDI can be used in at least three different scenarios:

1. *Public.* This is the scenario that's most talked about, and consists of a collection of replicating UDDI servers hosted by Microsoft, IBM, and HP. Anyone can obtain an account and perform inquiry and publish operations. Companies wishing to publish general-purpose web services use this public Internet UDDI system.

2. *Protected.* Some industry consortiums might wish to maintain their own UDDI servers that are specific to their industry, for performance or security reasons. If desired, these servers can be set up to replicate their content up to the public Internet UDDI system.

3. *Private.* Companies may choose to run internal UDDI servers to catalog their internal web services. For example, a large manufacturing company could use a private UDDI server to publish all of its individual manufacturing services for use by its in-house applications. If desired, the private UDDI server can be set up to replicate some or all of its content to those of its partners.

Protected and private registries will be the most common types of registry in the early days, I believe, because companies tend to be more comfortable adopting new technology in environments that they control.

One interesting project that I heard about involves a large telecommunication company that is considering using web services for connecting all of its next-generation telephones. In one of the proposed designs, the main switching hub would contain a UDDI server, and each phone would contain web services that provide the basic phone functionality. When a phone is plugged in, it would register its web services with the UDDI server, allowing other subsystems to locate the phone at a later stage. This might not be the most common usage scenario, but it's certainly one of the coolest!

Entities

UDDI allows you to store and manipulate four main types of entities:

Business	A Business represents an owner of web services. It has a name, a unique key, zero or more *Services*, and an optional set of contacts, descriptions, categories, and identifiers. Categories and identifiers can be used to specify things like a business's NAICS (North American Industrial Classification System), UNSPSC (Universal Standard Products and Services Classification), and DUNS (Data Universal Numbering System) codes, which can be useful when performing searches.

Service	A Service represents a group of one or more web services. It has a name, a unique key, one *Binding Template* per web service, an optional set of descriptions and categories, and a Business that it is owned by.
Binding Template	A Binding Template represents a single web service, and contains all the information that is needed to locate and invoke the service. It has a unique key, an access point that indicates the URL of the web service, an optional description, and a *TModel* key for each WSDL type that the web service implements.
TModel	A TModel represents a concept, from something as concrete as "the type specified by SimpleStockQuote.wsdl" to something as abstract as "the NAICS categorization scheme." A TModel has a name, a unique key, an overview URL that points to data associated with the TModel, and an optional set of descriptions. UDDI uses TModels for several different purposes, but their main use is for representing WSDL interface types. By allocating a unique TModel to each WSDL type, UDDI allows web services to be located based on the set of operations that they provide.

As an illustration, let's say that an industry consortium creates a standard WSDL for a credit checking service, and wishes to publish it so that companies can implement web services that support the standard. They would store the WSDL file at a public location like http://www.credit.org/CreditCheck.wsdl and publish a TModel for the WSDL interface definition at an operator node. The UDDI registry would allocate it a unique TModel key and store the address of the WSDL into the TModel overview URL (see Figure 6.1).

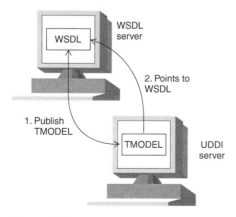

FIGURE 6.1
The consortium publishes a TModel for the credit checking WSDL

Members of the consortium that want to host a web service that implements the standard WSDL would publish their Business to an operator node. Then they would publish a Service with a single Binding Template whose access point is the URL of their web service implementation and whose TModel key is that of the credit checking TModel (see Figure 6.2).

Developers that wish to incorporate a credit checking web service into their application would first use a tool to browse the registry and obtain its TModel key. Then they can either select a specific implementation from the registry at development time, or use the UDDI inquiry API to select an implementation of the service at run time. In this run-time scenario, a client could cache the locations of more than one candidate service so that if one fails, another could automatically be swapped in as a replacement (see Figure 6.3).

In the short term, I think that most web services will be statically selected at development time. As a wider range of web services becomes available and the standards provide better support for quality of service, it will become more practical to select web services dynamically.

To understand how programs can take advantage of UDDI, let's take a closer look at the UDDI API.

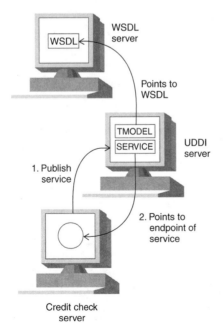

FIGURE 6.2
A member publishes a service to the UDDI server

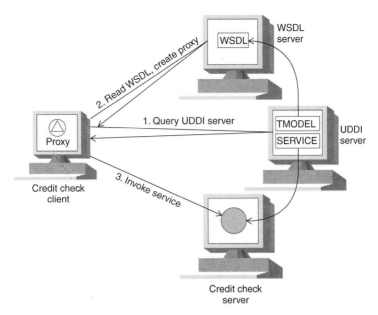

FIGURE 6.3
A client browses UDDI, reads the WSDL, creates a proxy, invokes the service

The UDDI API

The UDDI API is split into two parts, one for inquiring and one for publishing.

1. Inquiry methods allow entities to be retrieved based on their name, key, or other criteria. Each UDDI entity type (Business, Service, Binding, TModel) has a find_XXX method that returns a summary list of all the entities that match a criterion, and a get_XXX method that returns the details of a specific entity. A SOAP client typically invokes inquiry methods over a nonsecure HTTP connection.

2. Publish methods allow entities to be created, modified, and deleted. Each UDDI entity type (Business, Service, Binding, TModel) has a save_XXX method that adds an entity or replaces one, and a delete_XXX method that removes an entity. A SOAP client typically invokes publish methods over a secure HTTPS connection. To perform publish operations, you must first obtain an account on the UDDI server and get a user ID and password. All publish operations must include this user ID and password, and you can only modify and delete

entities that you created. Most public UDDI servers set limits on the number of entities of each type you can store, typically 1 Business per account, 4 Services per Business, 2 Binding Templates per Service, and 10 TModels per account.

The main UDDI web site, http://www.uddi.org, contains links to the UDDI specifications as well as the latest UDDI news.

A UDDI method invocation on the wire looks a lot like the other SOAP calls that we examined earlier. UDDI uses document-style invocation, so there are no xsi:type attributes with the SOAP parameters.

For example, here's the SOAP request and response for a UDDI find_business invocation to find businesses called Acme Credit. In this case, the result is a single Business with two Services, one for stock quotes and one for credit checks. The generic attribute is used to indicate the UDDI version.

UDDI Request

```
<?xml version='1.0' encoding='UTF-8'?>
<Envelope xmlns='http://schemas.xmlsoap.org/soap/envelope/'>
  <Body>
    <find_business generic='1.0' xmlns='urn:uddi-org:api'>
      <name>Acme Credit</name>
    </find_business>
  </Body>
</Envelope>
```

UDDI Response

```
<?xml version="1.0" encoding="UTF-8" ?>
<Envelope xmlns='http://schemas.xmlsoap.org/soap/envelope/'>
  <Body>
    <businessList
      generic='1.0'
      xmlns='urn:uddi-org:api'
      operator='www.ibm.com/services/uddi'
      truncated='false'>
      <businessInfos>
        <businessInfo businessKey='BA744ED0-3AAF-11D5-80DC-
002035229C64'>
          <name>Acme Credit</name>
          <description xml:lang='en'>Financial web services</
description>
          <serviceInfos>
            <serviceInfo
              serviceKey='D5B180A0-4342-11D5-BD6C-002035229C64'
              businessKey='BA744ED0-3AAF-11D5-80DC-002035229C64'>
```

```
            <name>Stock Quotes</name>
          </serviceInfo>
          <serviceInfo
            serviceKey='ED85F000-4345-11D5-BD6C-002035229C64'
            businessKey='BA744ED0-3AAF-11D5-80DC-002035229C64'>
            <name>Credit Checking</name>
          </serviceInfo>
        </serviceInfos>
      </businessInfo>
    </businessInfos>
  </businessList>
</Body>
</Envelope>
```

Toolkits are available which allow you to perform UDDI invocations from your favorite language, so you don't have to worry about knowing the XML message formats.

The next few sections delve into the details of inquiry and publish operations.

UDDI Registries

The examples in the next two sections use the IBM UDDI production registry, although they work fine with other UDDI registries as well. For reference, here are URLS for the public UDDI web sites and their endpoint addresses:

IBM production registry	Web site: https://www-3.ibm.com/services/uddi/protect/registry.html Inquiry endpoint: http://www-3.ibm.com/services/uddi/inquiryapi Publish endpoint: https://www-3.ibm.com/services/uddi/protect/publishapi
IBM test registry	Web site: https://www-3.ibm.com/services/uddi/testregistry/protect/registry.html Inquiry endpoint: http://www-3.ibm.com/services/uddi/testregistry/inquiryapi Publish endpoint: https://www-3.ibm.com/services/uddi/testregistry/protect/publishapi

Microsoft production registry	Web site: http://uddi.microsoft.com Inquiry endpoint: http://uddi.microsoft.com/inquire Publish endpoint: https://uddi.microsoft.com/publish
Microsoft test registry	Web site: http://test.uddi.microsoft.com Inquiry endpoint: http://test.uddi.microsoft.com/inquire Publish endpoint: https://test.uddi.microsoft.com/publish

Inquiring

This section describes how UDDI inquiry operations can be used to search for services via a browser, and used by SOAP clients to invoke web services that satisfy a particular criterion.

First, let's look at how you can use a browser to drill down into a UDDI registry.

Although each UDDI operator site provides a browser-based interface for searching their specific registry, I've found their interfaces to be lacking in detail. Fortunately, a tool by a company called SQLData Systems Inc. allows you to browse any UDDI registry from your browser and obtain a fine-grained level of information.

To use the tool, enter the URL http://www.soapclient.com/uddisearch.html into a browser. You are prompted to select the operator site and the search criteria. Then press SEARCH.

In this example (see Figure 6.4), I searched for all businesses called XMethods stored in the IBM UDDI registry. Because the public registries regularly synchronize, the search produces the same results if performed against the Microsoft or HP sites.

The search results include the business name, description and unique business key. Keys are usually 128-bit globally unique identifiers. Figure 6.5 shows the match I got for XMethods.

To see the services that a company provides, click its business key. Behind the scenes, the SQLData server invokes the appropriate UDDI operations to satisfy the query, and returns the result to the browser. I'll show you how to call the APIs from Java later in this section.

Figure 6.6 shows what I found when I clicked the XMethods business key. Notice that each service has a name, a unique service key, and a business key that refers to its owner.

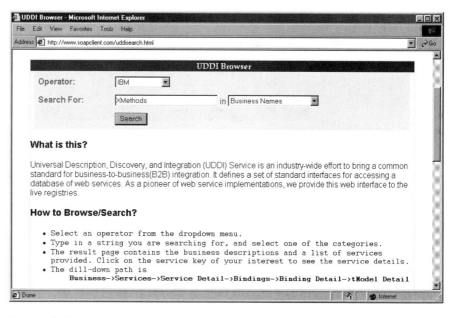

FIGURE 6.4
A search of the IBM UDDI registry

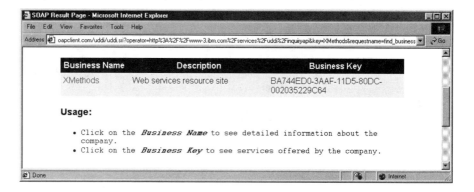

FIGURE 6.5
Details of search for XMethods

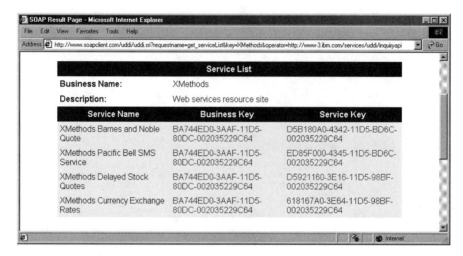

FIGURE 6.6
A list of services

To see more information about a particular service, click on its key. The name, description, access point, and binding template key are all displayed. Figure 6.7 shows what I got when I clicked the XMethods stock quotes service.

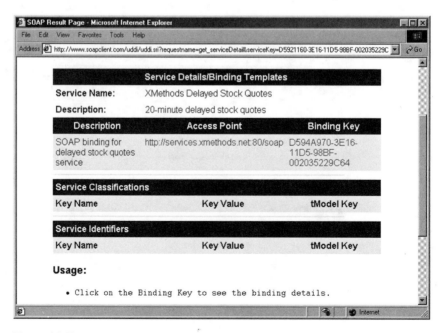

FIGURE 6.7
The XMethods stock quotes service

A service can have optional category and identifier tags that can assist in fine-grained searches. In this example, the stock quote service had neither.

To see the binding template details (see Figure 6.8), click the binding template key. You will see its description, TModel key and other miscellaneous information.

The XMethods stock quote service is thus an implementation of the WSDL interface defined by the TModel whose key is `UUID:0E727DB0-3E14-11D5-98BF-002035229C64`.

To see information about the TModel, click on its key. The TModel details page (see Figure 6.9) contains the name, description, and overview URL of the TModel, as well as its categories and identifiers. In this example, the overview URL points to the WSDL interface file, and the TModel is categorized as a "wsdlSpec" (WSDL specification).

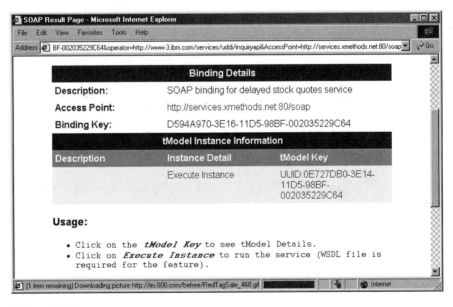

FIGURE 6.8
The binding details

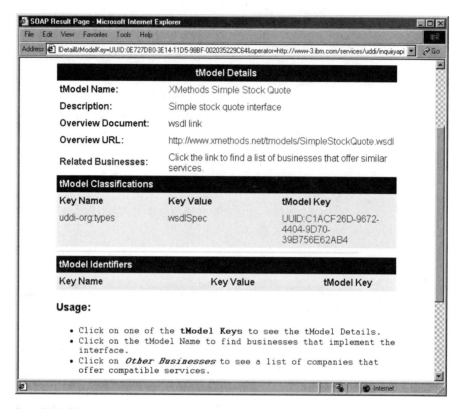

FIGURE 6.9
The TModel details page

To see the contents of the WSDL interface file, click the overview URL. Notice that because the WSDL defines an interface rather than an implementation, it does not contain a `<service>` entry.

Figure 6.10 shows the WSDL at http://www.xmethods.net/tmodels/SimpleStockQuote.wsdl.

Now that you've seen how UDDI inquiry operations can be performed via a browser, let's take a look at how the same operations can be performed from a SOAP client.

Here is the code for a UDDI client that obtains a summary of all businesses whose name matches the first command line argument. The program obtains a proxy to the UDDI inquiry service at the IBM operator site by passing its URL to the UDDIClient constructor. `findBusinesses()` takes the name of the business and an optional qualifier, and returns a summary of the businesses that match. The search qualifier, which in this example is omitted and set to null, can be used to specify the kind of match (exact, case sensitive) and the order that results are returned (ascending, descending).

FIGURE 6.10
The WSDL interface file

wsbook\src\book\uddi\Inquire1.java

```java
package book.uddi;

import electric.uddi.*;
import electric.uddi.client.*;

public class Inquire1
  {
  public static void main( String[] args )
    throws Exception
    {
    String businessName = args[ 0 ]; // first command line argument

    // create inquire-only connection to UDDI server
```

```
    String inquireURL = "http://www-3.ibm.com/services/uddi/
inquiryapi";
    IUDDI uddi = new UDDIClient( inquireURL );

    // get summaries of all businesses with specified name
    BusinessInfos businessInfos = uddi.findBusinesses( businessName,
null );

    // display summaries
    for( int i = 0; i < businessInfos.list.length; i++ )
      System.out.println( businessInfos.list[ i ] );
    }
  }
```

To run this example, execute Inquire1 with the name of the business as a command line argument. If the name contains spaces, surround it with quotes. Here is what I saw when looking for XMethods. Notice that the information is the same as the data that was displayed in the SQLData tool.

```
> java book.uddi.Inquire1 XMethods
<BusinessInfo>
  <businessInfo businessKey='BA744ED0-3AAF-11D5-80DC-002035229C64'>
    <name>XMethods</name>
    <description xml:lang='en'>Web services resource site</
description>
    <serviceInfos>
      <serviceInfo
        serviceKey='D5B180A0-4342-11D5-BD6C-002035229C64'
        businessKey='BA744ED0-3AAF-11D5-80DC-002035229C64'>
        <name>XMethods Barnes and Noble Quote</name>
      </serviceInfo>
      <serviceInfo
        serviceKey='ED85F000-4345-11D5-BD6C-002035229C64'
        businessKey='BA744ED0-3AAF-11D5-80DC-002035229C64'>
        <name>XMethods Pacific Bell SMS Service</name>
      </serviceInfo>
      <serviceInfo
        serviceKey='D5921160-3E16-11D5-98BF-002035229C64'
        businessKey='BA744ED0-3AAF-11D5-80DC-002035229C64'>
        <name>XMethods Delayed Stock Quotes</name>
      </serviceInfo>
      <serviceInfo
        serviceKey='618167A0-3E64-11D5-98BF-002035229C64'
        businessKey='BA744ED0-3AAF-11D5-80DC-002035229C64'>
        <name>XMethods Currency Exchange Rates</name>
      </serviceInfo>
    </serviceInfos>
  </businessInfo>
</BusinessInfo>
> _
```

The business summaries returned by findBusinesses() contain only the business key and service keys. To obtain detailed information about a particular business, use getBusiness () instead. The following example uses getBusiness() to obtain details about the first business returned by findBusinesses(), essentially performing a "drilldown" operation.

wsbook\src\book\uddi\Inquire2.java

```
package book.uddi;

import electric.uddi.*;
import electric.uddi.client.*;

public class Inquire2
  {
  public static void main( String[] args )
    throws Exception
    {
    String businessName = args[ 0 ]; // first command line argument

    // create inquire-only connection to UDDI server
    String inquireURL = "http://www-3.ibm.com/services/uddi/inquiryapi";
    IUDDI uddi = new UDDIClient( inquireURL );

    // get summaries of all businesses with specified name
    BusinessInfos businessInfos = uddi.findBusinesses( businessName,
null );

    // get and print first business with specified name
    String key = businessInfos.list[ 0 ].getBusinessKey();
    Business business = uddi.getBusiness( key );
    System.out.println( business );
    }
  }
```

To run the example, execute Inquire2 with the name of the business as a command line argument. Here are the details about XMethods that were returned. Note that the business service entry for the delayed stock quote service includes an accessPoint element equal to http://services.xmethods.net:80/soap, which is the address of its SOAP endpoint, and a TModel key of UUID:0E727DB0-3E14-11D5-98BF-002035229C64.

```
> java book.uddi.Inquire2 XMethods
<Business>
  <businessEntity
    businessKey='BA744ED0-3AAF-11D5-80DC-002035229C64'
    authorizedName='0100001QS1'
    operator='www.ibm.com/services/uddi'>
    <discoveryURLs>
      <discoveryURL useType='businessEntity'>http://www.ibm.com/
services/uddi/
```

```
uddiget?businessKey=BA744ED0-3AAF-11D5-80DC-002035229C64</
discoveryURL>
      <discoveryURL useType='businessEntity'>http://www-3.ibm.
com/services/uddi/uddiget?businessKey=A94E0DD0-1084-11D5-8C37-
AE8C32CC1A0A</discoveryURL>
    </discoveryURLs>
    <name>XMethods</name>
    <description xml:lang='en'>Web services resource site</description>
    <contacts>
      <contact useType='Founder'>
        <description xml:lang='en'/>
        <personName>Tony Hong</personName>
        <phone useType='Founder'/>
        <email useType='Founder'>thong@xmethods.net</email>
        <address>
          <addressLine/>
          <addressLine/>
          <addressLine/>
          <addressLine/>
          <addressLine/>
        </address>
      </contact>
    </contacts>
    <businessServices>
      <businessService
        serviceKey='D5921160-3E16-11D5-98BF-002035229C64'
        businessKey='BA744ED0-3AAF-11D5-80DC-002035229C64'>
        <name>XMethods Delayed Stock Quotes</name>
        <description xml:lang='en'>20-minute delayed stock quotes</
description>
        <bindingTemplates>
          <bindingTemplate
            bindingKey='D594A970-3E16-11D5-98BF-002035229C64'
            serviceKey='D5921160-3E16-11D5-98BF-002035229C64'>
            <description xml:lang='en'>SOAP binding for delayed
              stock quotes service</description>
            <accessPoint
              URLType='http'>http://services.xmethods.net:80/soap
            </accessPoint>
            <tModelInstanceDetails>
              <tModelInstanceInfo
                tModelKey='UUID:0E727DB0-3E14-11D5-98BF-002035229C64'/>
            </tModelInstanceDetails>
          </bindingTemplate>
        </bindingTemplates>
      </businessService>

    … other business services omitted for brevity

    </businessServices>
  </businessEntity>
</Business>
> _
```

The next example uses getTModel() to retrieve information about the
TModel for delayed stock quotes.

wsbook\src\book\uddi\Inquire3.java

```
package book.uddi;

import electric.uddi.*;
import electric.uddi.client.*;

public class Inquire3
  {
  public static void main( String[] args )
    throws Exception
    {
    // tModel key for Stock Quotes interface
    String tModelKey = "UUID:0E727DB0-3E14-11D5-98BF-002035229C64";

    // create inquire-only connection to UDDI server
    String inquireURL = "http://www-3.ibm.com/services/uddi/inquiryapi";
    IUDDI uddi = new UDDIClient( inquireURL );

    // get tModel with specified key
    TModel tModel = uddi.getTModel( tModelKey );
    System.out.println( tModel );
    }
  }
```

To run the example, execute Inquire3. Here is what you should see. Note
that the TModel overview URL points to the WSDL for the delayed stock
quotes interface.

```
> java book.uddi.Inquire3
<TModel>
  <tModel
    tModelKey='UUID:0E727DB0-3E14-11D5-98BF-002035229C64'
    authorizedName='0100001QS1'
    operator='www.ibm.com/services/uddi'>
    <name>XMethods Simple Stock Quote</name>
    <description xml:lang='en'>Simple stock quote interface</description>
    <overviewDoc>
      <description xml:lang='en'>wsdl link</description>
      <overviewURL>
        http://www.xmethods.net/tmodels/SimpleStockQuote.wsdl
      </overviewURL>
    </overviewDoc>
    <categoryBag>
      <keyedReference
        keyName='uddi-org:types'
        keyValue='wsdlSpec'
        tModelKey='UUID:C1ACF26D-9672-4404-9D70-39B756E62AB4'/>
```

```
    </categoryBag>
  </tModel>
</TModel>
> _
```

The UDDI inquiry API includes a method for finding all businesses with a service that implements a particular set of interfaces/TModels. In the publish section of this chapter, I'll show you how to register a service of your own that implements a particular TModel.

The following example uses findBusinesses() to find all businesses that implement the stock quote TModel.

wsbook\src\book\uddi\Inquire4.java

```java
package book.uddi;

import electric.uddi.*;
import electric.uddi.client.*;

public class Inquire4
   {
  public static void main( String[] args )
    throws Exception
    {
    // tModel key for Stock Quotes interface
    String tModelKey = "UUID:0E727DB0-3E14-11D5-98BF-002035229C64";

    // create inquire-only connection to UDDI server
    String inquireURL = "http://www-3.ibm.com/services/uddi/inquiryapi";
    IUDDI uddi = new UDDIClient( inquireURL );

    // get summaries of all businesses with specified tModel
    String[] tModelKeys = new String[]{ tModelKey };
    BusinessInfos businessInfos = uddi.findBusinesses( tModelKeys, null );

    // display list of businesses
    for( int i = 0; i < businessInfos.list.length; i++ )
      System.out.println( businessInfos.list[ i ].getName() );
    }
  }
```

To run the example, execute Inquire4. As you can see from the output, XMethods was the only business that currently implemented the service at the time I ran the example. When you run it, you may see more businesses listed, perhaps published by readers of this book!

```
> java book.uddi.Inquire4
XMethods
> _
```

Now it's time for the fun part, namely using UDDI to dynamically locate a web service according to a particular set of criteria. In this case, the client program selects and invokes the first web service that is owned by a particular company and implements the stock quotes TModel.

Before writing the Java client that binds to the web service, it's necessary to generate a Java interface that corresponds to the stock quote TModel. The simplest way to do this is to invoke the wsdl2java command line utility from the wsbook\src\book\uddi directory as follows:

```
> wsdl2java http://www.xmethods.net/tmodels/SimpleStockQuote.wsdl -p
examples.uddi
write file IStockQuotePortType.java
>
```

The following UDDI client finds a business with a name that matches the first command line argument and then finds the first service owned by that business that implements the stock quote interface/TModel. Next, it passes the URL of the TModel WSDL to `Registry.bind()`, passing in the web service endpoint as a Context property and receiving back a proxy to the specified implementation of the stock quote interface. Finally, it uses the proxy to invoke the web service. See the GLUE user guide for more information about Context objects and how to use them.

wsbook\src\book\uddi\Inquire5.java

```java
package book.uddi;

import electric.util.Context;
import electric.uddi.*;
import electric.uddi.client.*;
import electric.registry.Registry;

public class Inquire5
  {
  public static void main( String[] args )
    throws Exception
    {
    String businessName = args[ 0 ]; // first command line argument
```

```
    // tModel key for Stock Quotes interface
    String tModelKey = "UUID:0E727DB0-3E14-11D5-98BF-002035229C64";
    String inquireURL = "http://www-3.ibm.com/services/uddi/
inquiryapi";

    // create inquire-only connection to UDDI server
    IUDDI uddi = new UDDIClient( inquireURL );

    // get the key of the business
    BusinessInfos businessInfos = uddi.findBusinesses( businessName,
null );
    String businessKey = businessInfos.list[ 0 ].getBusinessKey();

    // get the URL of the WSDL for the service interface from the
tModel
    TModel tModel = uddi.getTModel( tModelKey );
    String wsdl = tModel.getOverview().getOverviewURL();
    System.out.println( "wsdl = " + wsdl );

    // get first service that the business provides that implements
the tModel
    String[] tModelKeys = new String[]{ tModelKey };
    ServiceInfos serviceInfos = uddi.findServices( businessKey,
tModelKeys, null );
    String serviceKey = serviceInfos.list[ 0 ].getServiceKey();
    Service service = uddi.getService( serviceKey );

    // get the endpoint from the service binding
    Binding binding = service.getBindings()[ 0 ];
    AccessPoint accessPoint = binding.getAccessPoint();
    String endpoint = accessPoint.getAddress();
    System.out.println( "endpoint = " + endpoint );

    // bind to service that implements WSDL at the specified endpoint
    Context context = new Context();
    context.setProperty( "endpoint", endpoint );
    IStockQuotePortType stockQuotes = (IStockQuotePortType)
      Registry.bind( wsdl, IStockQuotePortType.class, context );

    // invoke the service via a java interface
    float quote1 = stockQuotes.getQuote( "IBM" );
    System.out.println( "stock price of IBM = " + quote1 );

    // invoke the service via a java interface
    float quote2 = stockQuotes.getQuote( "MSFT" );
    System.out.println( "stock price of MSFT = " + quote2 );
    }
  }
```

To invoke a stock quote web service that's owned by XMethods, execute Inquire5 with XMethods as the command line argument. The output displays the URL of the WSDL (found from the TModel), the endpoint of the web service (found from the service's binding template), and the results of invoking the web service.

```
> java book.uddi.Inquire5 XMethods
wsdl = http://www.xmethods.net/tmodels/SimpleStockQuote.wsdl
endpoint = http://services.xmethods.net:80/soap
stock price of IBM = 117.5
stock price of MSFT = 72.36
> _
```

It would be relatively easy to modify Inquire5 to use findBusinesses() to locate all the businesses that implement a stock quotes service, use find-Services() to get the stock quotes service from each of these businesses, and then select one based on a particular set of criteria.

Now that you've seen how the UDDI inquiry API can be used to locate and bind to web services, it's time to explore the publish API.

Publishing

This section describes how UDDI publish operations can be used to register businesses and their web services. The first part explains the process of obtaining a UDDI account and manually registering your business using a browser. The second part shows how a SOAP client can programmatically publish a service using the UDDI API.

If you want to execute the examples in this section, you must first obtain a UDDI account. To do this, visit one of the following operator sites:

- IBM—http://www-3.ibm.com/services/uddi/
- Microsoft—http://uddi.microsoft.com/

Each site provides instructions on how to obtain an account from the operator company. After entering basic information about your company, including a user ID and password, you are sent an activation code which you must enter the first time you log on. After that, you can inquire and publish from either a browser or a SOAP client.

In this example, I obtained an account from the IBM site. Once my account was activated, the first thing I did was to register my business. Although this could be done programmatically via the SOAP APIs, I used the browser to demonstrate what an operator site user interface looks like.

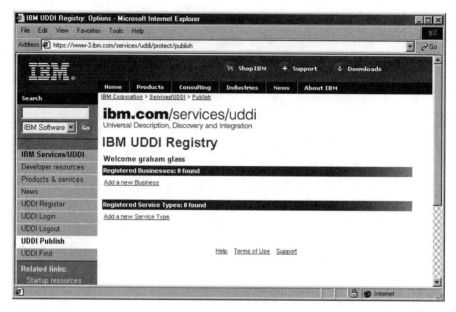

FIGURE 6.11
The IBM welcome page

Figure 6.11 is the IBM welcome page that allows you to add new businesses and TModels (which IBM calls *service types*).

To add a business, click the appropriate link. You should see the page in Figure 6.12.

For this example, I entered Acme Quotes (a ficticious company) as the name of the business and then pressed Continue. You should pick an unusual name of your own.

The next screen (see Figure 6.13) presents a host of options for adding descriptions, contacts, and categories (which IBM calls *locators*).

In this example, I entered a short description of the business and a contact called Harry Potter (financial wizard). The resulting business page looked like the one in Figure 6.14.

FIGURE 6.12
The add a business page

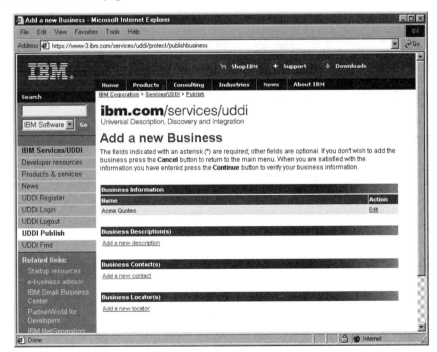

FIGURE 6.13
Options for adding a business

FIGURE 6.14
The business name and contact

To classify your business, click the "add a new locator" link. This takes you to a page that allows you to classify your business according to one of three industry standard classification systems. In this example (see Figure 6.15), I selected UNSPS.

Depending on which scheme you choose (you can select more than one if you like), you're guided through a classification process and end up with a code that denotes your business type. In Figure 6.16, I ended up with the UNSPSC code 84121801, which stands for "Stock market trading services."

At this point, the registration of the business is complete. Verify that the business was added by performing a name search using the SQLData UDDI browser. When you find the business, make a note of its key for use in the next section. In my case, Acme Quotes was allocated the business key 69D5C330-5ACD-11D5-92D3-002035229C64.

The next step is to register a web service using the UDDI publish API.

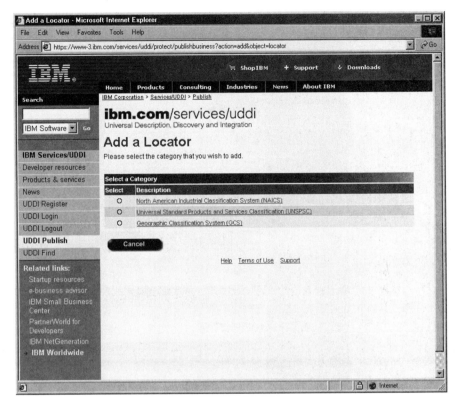

FIGURE 6.15
Choosing a classification

FIGURE 6.16
Business code assignment

To illustrate the concept of binding dynamically to one of potentially many implementations of a web service, let's publish a web service that implements the same WSDL interface as the XMethods Stock Quotes service.

The StockQuotes class is a simple implementation of the IStockQuote-PortType interface that we previously generated using wsdl2java.

wsbook\src\book\uddi\StockQuotes.java

```
package book.uddi;

/**
 * Demo implementation of IStockQuotePortType
 */
public class StockQuotes implements IStockQuotePortType
  {
  public float getQuote( String symbol )
```

```
    {
    return 42; // hard coded for demo purposes
    }
}
```

The StockQuotesServer program publishes a stock quotes web service on port 8004 of the local host.

wsbook\src\book\uddi\StockQuotesServer.java

```
package book.uddi;

import electric.registry.Registry;
import electric.server.http.HTTP;

public class StockQuotesServer
  {
  public static void main( String[] args )
    throws Exception
    {
    // start a web server on port 8004, accept messages via /soap
    HTTP.startup( "http://localhost:8004/soap" );

    // publish an instance of StockQuotes
    Registry.publish( "quotes", new StockQuotes() );
    }
  }
```

To use the publish APIs, you must create an authenticating client to the UDDI server that uses the user ID and password that you obtained from the UDDI operator site. To do this using GLUE, construct a UDDIClient with the inquiry URL, publish URL, user ID, and password. The first time you perform a publish operation, the client authenticates using the user ID and password, and then automatically transmits the resulting authentication token with every subsequent publish operation.

The following example creates a Service with a Binding that implements the stock quote TModel and specifies http://199.174.20.70:8004/soap/quotes as its access point. It then uses saveService() to upload the service into the IBM UDDI registry, and displays the Service that was saved.

Before running the example, replace the businessKey with the key of your own business, which you can find using the SQLData UDDI browsing tool. Also replace the accessPoint IP address with the IP address of your own local host, and supply the user name and password given to you by the IBM UDDI site.

wsbook\src\book\uddi\Publish1.java

```java
package book.uddi;

import electric.uddi.*;
import electric.uddi.client.*;

public class Publish1
   {
  public static void main( String[] args )
    throws Exception
    {
    // tModel key for Stock Quotes interface
    String tModelKey = "UUID:0E727DB0-3E14-11D5-98BF-002035229C64";

    // business key of Acme Quotes - replace with your own key
    String businessKey = "69D5C330-5ACD-11D5-92D3-002035229C64";

    // create inquire/publish connection to UDDI server, with
authentication
    String inquireURL = "http://www-3.ibm.com/services/uddi/
inquiryapi";
    String publishURL = "https://www-3.ibm.com/services/uddi/protect/
publishapi";
    // replace user name and password with your own.
    IUDDI uddi = new UDDIClient( inquireURL, publishURL,
"acmequotes", "xxxx" );

    // create service, set its business key
    Service service = new Service( "stock quotes" );
    service.setBusinessKey( businessKey );

    // create binding, set its tModel and access point
    Binding binding = new Binding();
    binding.addDescription( new Description( "SOAP binding for Stock
Quotes type" ) );
    TModelInstance tModelInstance = new TModelInstance( tModelKey );
    binding.addTModelInstance( tModelInstance );
    // replace IP address with your own.
    AccessPoint accessPoint = new AccessPoint( "http://
199.174.20.70:8004/soap/quotes", "http" );
    binding.setAccessPoint( accessPoint );

    // add binding to service
    service.addBinding( binding );

    // save the service
    Service savedService = uddi.saveService( service );
    System.out.println( savedService );
    }
  }
```

To run the example, execute Publish1. You should see the following kind of output, but with your own keys and access point.

```
> java book.uddi.Publish1
<Service>
  <businessService
    serviceKey='44FCB4E0-5B24-11D5-92D3-002035229C64'
    businessKey='69D5C330-5ACD-11D5-92D3-002035229C64'>
    <name>stock quotes</name>
    <bindingTemplates>
      <bindingTemplate
        bindingKey='44FD9F40-5B24-11D5-92D3-002035229C64'
        serviceKey='44FCB4E0-5B24-11D5-92D3-002035229C64'>
        <description xml:lang='en'>
          SOAP binding for Stock Quotes type
        </description>
        <accessPoint URLType='http'>
          http://199.174.20.70:8004/soap/quotes
        </accessPoint>
        <tModelInstanceDetails>
          <tModelInstanceInfo
            tModelKey='UUID:0E727DB0-3E14-11D5-98BF-002035229C64'/>
        </tModelInstanceDetails>
      </bindingTemplate>
    </bindingTemplates>
  </businessService>
</Service>
> _
```

After executing the example, use the SQLData UDDI browser to confirm that your service had been published. In this case, I searched for Acme Credit and then clicked its stock quotes service link. Figure 6.17 is what I saw.

The binding key links to a page that shows the TModel key for the service, which in this case is the same TModel key that is implemented by the XMethods stock quote service (see Figure 6.18).

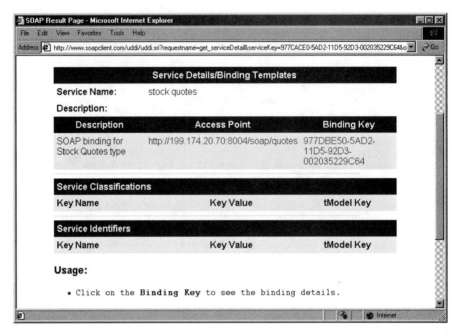

FIGURE 6.17
Our published service

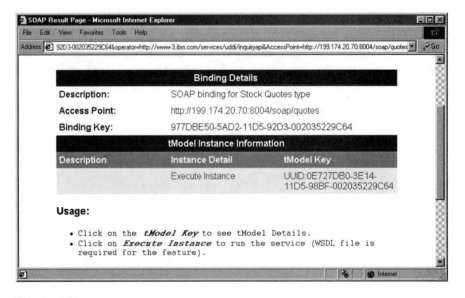

FIGURE 6.18
Binding details

If you run Inquire4 again, you'll see your own company in the list of businesses that implement the stock quote interfaces. In my case, I saw Acme Quotes in the following list:

```
> java book.uddi.Inquire4
Acme Quotes
XMethods
> _
```

When Inquire5 was run again with "Acme Quotes" as the business whose Stock Quotes service should be used, it invoked the web service running on the StockQuotesServer.

```
> java book.uddi.Inquire5 "Acme Quotes"
wsdl = http://www.xmethods.net/tmodels/SimpleStockQuote.wsdl
endpoint = http://199.174.20.70:8004/soap/quotes
stock price of IBM = 42
stock price of MSFT = 42
> _
```

There is a handy UDDI API that allows you to see all of the businesses and TModels that you published. The following program uses `getRegistered()` to display a summary list of the businesses that I created, together with their service keys.

wsbook\src\book\uddi\Publish2.java

```java
package book.uddi;

import electric.uddi.*;
import electric.uddi.client.*;

public class Publish2
  {
  public static void main( String[] args )
    throws Exception
    {
    // create inquire/publish connection to UDDI server, with
authentication
    String inquireURL = "http://www-3.ibm.com/services/uddi/
inquiryapi";
    String publishURL = "https://www-3.ibm.com/services/uddi/protect/
publishapi";
    IUDDI uddi = new UDDIClient( inquireURL, publishURL,
"acmequotes", "xxxx" );
```

```
    // get information about the user's registered entities
    Registered registered = uddi.getRegistered();
    BusinessInfo[] businessInfos = registered.getBusinessInfos();

    // display summaries of all businesses associated with this user/
password
    for( int i = 0; i < businessInfos.length; i++ )
       System.out.println( "businessInfo " + i + " =\n" +
businessInfos[ i ] );
    }
  }
```

To run the example, execute Publish2. You should see the following kind of output, but with your own business and service keys.

```
> java book.uddi.Publish2
businessInfo 0 =
<BusinessInfo>
  <businessInfo businessKey='69D5C330-5ACD-11D5-92D3-002035229C64'>
    <name>Acme Quotes</name>
    <description xml:lang='en'>
      provides a variety of stock quote services
    </description>
    <serviceInfos>
      <serviceInfo
        serviceKey='977CACE0-5AD2-11D5-92D3-002035229C64'
        businessKey='69D5C330-5ACD-11D5-92D3-002035229C64'>
        <name>stock quotes</name>
      </serviceInfo>
    </serviceInfos>
  </businessInfo>
</BusinessInfo>
> _
```

The Future of UDDI

UDDI is evolving fairly rapidly. Version 2 has new features for representing business relationships and performing more sophisticated searches. In addition, the protocol for replicating information between UDDI registries was documented, allowing third parties to potentially form their own operator clouds.

UDDI is an interesting blend between a web services discovery system and a business information registry. There is a danger that if both sets of functionality continue to grow, UDDI will become too complex for use as a general purpose mechanism for web service discovery and a new standard will have to take its place. My personal prefence would be for the discovery and business information functions to be teased apart into separate APIs that could evolve independently.

It's possible that research by the P2P community into distributed search mechanisms will influence the evolution of UDDI. Chapter 10 describes some of the P2P work that could allow large-scale distributed implementations of UDDI.

Summary

In this chapter, we started by looking at three different usage scenarios for UDDI. Then we listed the entities that are stored into a UDDI registry and saw how they would be involved in a simple credit checking system. Finally, we used the inquiry and published APIs to access and modify the contents of the IBM UDDI registry.

Quiz

- What is the purpose of classifying a business using an industry standard classification system?
- How can a program dynamically select an implementation of a particular service type?

Exercises

1. Why do you think UDDI doesn't use HTTP basic authentication for its security system?
2. What is the point of securing publish operations?
3. Run the examples against the Microsoft UDDI Registry and confirm they yield the same result.
4. Could you replace UDDI with a system that publishes descriptive web services pages to Yahoo!?
5. Why do you think the UDDI architects used TModels instead of XML namespaces?
6. What do you think the term TModel stands for?

J2EE Web Services

7

J2EE is the umbrella term for a set of Java technologies that allow developers to create secure, scaleable, portable, commercial-quality applications. This chapter shows how J2EE supports the development and deployment of web services, and how J2EE clients can invoke web services deployed on other platforms.

I chose BEA WebLogic 6.1 as the implementation platform because it is popular and easy to install. Similar functionality is available from products such as IBM WebSphere, Sun iPlanet, and HP Bluestone.

Overview

J2EE is supported by a variety of vendors, and includes the following subsystems:

- EJB
- Servlets

- JSP (JavaServer Pages)
- RMI
- JMS (Java Messaging Service)
- JNDI (Java Naming and Directory Interface)
- JTA (Java Transaction API)
- JDBC (Java DataBase Connectivity)
- JavaMail

Developers who use J2EE to build applications are encouraged to package software services as EJBs, which come in a variety of flavors:

- *Stateless session beans*, short-term services that process a single request.
- *Stateful session beans*, medium-term services that process a series of requests associated with a particular session and can maintain state during this period.
- *Entity beans*, long-term services that represent a persistent entity that is typically stored in a relational database.
- *Message beans*, which provide integration with JMS messaging.

All J2EE containers provide RMI access to the EJBs that they host, and many containers also provide CORBA access. To accommodate the rise of web services, many J2EE vendors, including BEA and IBM, have integrated native support for web services standards into their offerings so that EJBs can be published using WSDL and accessed using SOAP.

The next few sections show how EJBs can be published and consumed as web services.

Installing J2EE

This chapter uses BEA WebLogic 6.1 as the example J2EE platform. You can download a free evaluation copy of WebLogic server from http://www.bea.com.

I installed my copy of WebLogic into a top-level directory called \bea, set my default domain to "mydomain," and set my system password to something suitable.

Publishing J2EE Web Services

To illustrate how an EJB can be published as a web service, let's create a stateless session bean that provides the familiar currency exchange service, host it in a J2EE server, and access it from a GLUE client using SOAP.

The stateless session bean for this example was built according to standard J2EE practices and doesn't contain any code that is specific to web services. The bean is comprised of a remote interface, a home interface, and an implementation class.

The IExchangeBean remote interface was modeled on the IExchange interface defined earlier in the book:

wsbook\src\book\j2ee\IExchangeBean.java

```
package book.j2ee;

import java.rmi.RemoteException;
import javax.ejb.EJBObject;

public interface IExchangeBean extends EJBObject
  {
  void setValue( String country, double value ) throws
RemoteException;
  double getValue( String country ) throws ExchangeException,
RemoteException;
  double getRate( String country1, String country2 ) throws
ExchangeException, RemoteException;
  }
```

Due to the immaturity of web services integration into J2EE, many vendors only support primitive data types as arguments and return values, although this restriction will quickly pass.

The ExchangeHome home interface is used by clients to create an instance of the stateless bean.

wsbook\src\book\j2ee\ExchangeHome.java

```
package book.j2ee;

import java.rmi.RemoteException;
import javax.ejb.CreateException;
import javax.ejb.EJBHome;
```

```
public interface ExchangeHome extends EJBHome
  {
  IExchangeBean create() throws CreateException, RemoteException;
  }
```

The implementation of the stateless exchange bean was built according to J2EE standard practices, and stores the currency exchange values in a static Hashtable. A real system would of course keep these values in some kind of persistent store.

Note that the ExchangeBean does not implement IExchangeBean. This is intentional and in accordance with the J2EE specification.

wsbook\src\book\j2ee\ExchangeBean.java

```
package book.j2ee;

import java.util.*;
import javax.ejb.CreateException;
import javax.ejb.SessionBean;
import javax.ejb.SessionContext;
import javax.naming.InitialContext;
import javax.naming.NamingException;

public class ExchangeBean implements SessionBean
  {
  static Hashtable values = new Hashtable(); // currency values in US
dollars

  static
    {
    // initialize default values for demo
    values.put( "usa", new Double( 1 ) );
    values.put( "japan", new Double( 0.4 ) );
    }

  SessionContext context;

  // STANDARD EJB STATELESS SESSION BEAN METHODS

  public void setSessionContext( SessionContext context )
    {
    this.context = context;
    }

  public void ejbActivate()
    {
    }

  public void ejbRemove()
```

```
    {
    }

  public void ejbPassivate()
    {
    }

  public void ejbCreate ()
    throws CreateException
    {
    try
      {
      InitialContext initialContext = new InitialContext();
      }
    catch( NamingException exception )
      {
      throw new CreateException( "failed to find environment value "
+ exception );
      }
    }

  // DOMAIN-SPECIFIC METHODS

  public void setValue( String country, double value )
    {
    values.put( country, new Double( value ) );
    }

  public double getValue( String country )
    throws ExchangeException
    {
    Double value = (Double) values.get( country );

    if( value == null )
      throw new ExchangeException( "country " + country + " not
recognized" );

    return value.doubleValue();
    }

  public double getRate( String country1, String country2 )
    throws ExchangeException
    {
    return getValue( country1 ) / getValue( country2 );
    }
  }
```

To build an EJB, BEA recommends that you use Apache Ant. Ant is an intuitive, Java-based alternative to makefiles, and can be downloaded from http://jakarta.apache.org/ant/index.html.

Three build files are required to build the EJB defined by the previous three files. The first is the high-level build file that calls the other two.

wsbook\src\book\j2ee\build.xml

```
<project name="exchange" default="webservice">
  <target name="webservice">
    <ant dir="." antfile="build-ejb.xml"/>
    <ant dir="." antfile="build-ws.xml"/>
  </target>
</project>
```

The build-ejb.xml file calls the various WebLogic utilities for compiling and packaging the EJB.

wsbook\src\book\j2ee\build-ejb.xml

```
<project name="ejb-basic-statelessSession" default="all" basedir=".">
  <!-- set global properties for this build -->
  <property file="examples.properties"/>
  <property name="src" value="."/>
  <property name="build" value="${src}/build"/>
  <property name="dist" value="."/>
  <property name="WL_HOME" value=""/>

  <target name="all" depends="clean, init, compile_ejb, jar_ejb,
ejbc"/>

  <target name="init">
    <!-- Create the time stamp -->
    <tstamp/>
    <!-- Create the build directory structure used by compile and
copy the deployment descriptors into it-->
    <mkdir dir="${build}"/>
    <mkdir dir="${build}/META-INF"/>
    <copy todir="${build}/META-INF">
      <fileset dir="${src}">
        <include name="*.xml"/>
      </fileset>
    </copy>
  </target>

  <!-- Compile ejb classes into the build directory (jar preparation)
-->
  <target name="compile_ejb">
    <javac srcdir="${src}" destdir="${build}"
includes="IExchangeBean.java, ExchangeHome.java, ExchangeBean.java
ExchangeException.java"/>
  </target>
```

```
    <!-- Make a standard ejb jar file, including XML deployment
descriptors -->
    <target name="jar_ejb" depends="compile_ejb">
      <jar jarfile="${dist}/a_exchange.jar" basedir="${build}"></jar>
    </target>

    <!-- Run ejbc to create the deployable jar file -->
    <target name="ejbc" depends="jar_ejb">
      <java classname="weblogic.ejbc" fork="yes">
        <sysproperty key="weblogic.home" value="${WL_HOME}"/>
        <arg line="-compiler javac ${dist}/a_exchange.jar ./
exchange.jar"/>
        <classpath>
          <pathelement path="${WL_HOME}/lib/weblogic_sp.jar;${WL_HOME}/
lib/weblogic.jar"/>
        </classpath>
      </java>
    </target>

    <target name="clean">
      <delete dir="${build}"/>
    </target>
</project>
```

The build-ejb.xml file requires two additional files to be present:

- ejb-jar.xml, which describes the standard EJB characteristics
- weblogic-ejb-jar.xml, which describes WebLogic-specific characteristics

The ejb-jar.xml file specifies the EJB type, the Java classes that define it, and the transaction settings.

wsbook\src\book\j2ee\ejb-jar.xml

```
<?xml version="1.0"?>
<!DOCTYPE ejb-jar PUBLIC '-//Sun Microsystems, Inc.//DTD Enterprise
JavaBeans 1.1//EN' 'http://java.sun.com/j2ee/dtds/ejb-jar_1_1.dtd'>
<ejb-jar>
  <enterprise-beans>
    <session>
      <ejb-name>exchangeService</ejb-name>
      <home>book.j2ee.ExchangeHome</home>
      <remote>book.j2ee.IExchangeBean</remote>
      <ejb-class>book.j2ee.ExchangeBean</ejb-class>
      <session-type>Stateless</session-type>
      <transaction-type>Container</transaction-type>
    </session>
  </enterprise-beans>
  <assembly-descriptor>
    <container-transaction>
      <method>
```

```
            <ejb-name>exchangeService</ejb-name>
            <method-intf>Remote</method-intf>
            <method-name>*</method-name>
         </method>
         <trans-attribute>Required</trans-attribute>
      </container-transaction>
   </assembly-descriptor>
</ejb-jar>
```

The weblogic-ejb-jar.xml file includes information such as the JNDI name for the EJB and the maximum number of the stateless beans that should be pooled.

wsbook\src\book\j2ee\weblogic-ejb-jar.xml

```
<?xml version="1.0"?>
<!DOCTYPE weblogic-ejb-jar PUBLIC '-//BEA Systems, Inc.//DTD WebLogic
5.1.0 EJB//EN' 'http://www.bea.com/servers/wls510/dtd/weblogic-ejb-
jar.dtd'>
<weblogic-ejb-jar>
   <weblogic-enterprise-bean>
     <ejb-name>exchangeService</ejb-name>
     <caching-descriptor>
        <max-beans-in-free-pool>100</max-beans-in-free-pool>
     </caching-descriptor>
     <jndi-name>exchangeService.ExchangeHome</jndi-name>
   </weblogic-enterprise-bean>
</weblogic-ejb-jar>
```

The build-ws.xml file uses the WebLogic wsgen utility to create the additional files that allow the EJB to be accessed as a web service, and includes the name of the EJB to publish, together with the URI of the servlet that should accept incoming SOAP messages.

wsbook\src\book\j2ee\build-ws.xml

```
<project name="exchange-webservice" default="copy">
  <!-- set global properties for this build -->
  <property file="examples.properties"/>
  <property name="module" value="exchange"/>
  <property name="jar.path" value="${module}.jar"/>
  <property name="ear.path" value="${module}.ear"/>

  <target name="wsgen">
    <wsgen destpath="${ear.path}" context="/exchange"
host="localhost" port="7001">
      <rpcservices path="${jar.path}">
```

```
          <rpcservice bean="exchangeService" uri="/exchangeuri"/>
        </rpcservices>
      </wsgen>
    </target>

    <target name="copy" depends="wsgen">
      <copy file="${ear.path}" todir="${APPLICATIONS}"/>
    </target>

  </project>
```

To execute the build, type the following command from the wsbook\src\
book\j2ee directory:

```
> \bea\wlserver6.1\bin\ant
```

Here is the build output you should see:

```
Buildfile: build.xml

webservice:

clean:
    [delete] Deleting directory C:\BOOK\src\examples\build

init:
    [mkdir] Created dir: C:\BOOK\src\book\j2ee\build
    [mkdir] Created dir: C:\BOOK\src\book\j2ee\build\META-INF
    [copy] Copying 5 files to C:\BOOK\src\book\j2ee\build\META-INF

compile_ejb:
    [javac] Compiling 4 source files to C:\BOOK\src\book\j2ee\build

jar_ejb:
    [jar] Building jar: C:\BOOK\src\book\j2ee\a_exchange.jar

ejbc:

all:

wsgen:

copy:
    [copy] Copying 1 file to
    C:\bea\wlserver6.1\config\mydomain\applications

BUILD SUCCESSFUL

Total time: 20 seconds
```

The build process creates an enterprise application resource file called exchange.ear and copies it into \bea\wlserver6.1\config\mydomain\applications directory for automatic deployment. In this example, the file is about 140 KB and contains the following resources:

- **Manifest.mf**—the manifest that describes the contents of the .ear file
- **application.xml**—indicates the EJB file (exchange.jar), the web services file (web-services.war), and the context (/exchange)
- **exchange.jar**—the domain EJB classes, including ExchangeBean, IExchangeBean, and so forth
- **web-services.war**—contains the web-services specific files, including:
  - **weblogic.xml**, which defines the JDNI name for the web service
  - **web.xml**, which defines a special StatelessBeanAdapter servlet for the web service
  - **index.html**, which is the home page for the web service
  - **client.jar**, which is a self-contained .jar that gives Java clients access to the web service

If you wish to skip the build process for now, simply copy the pre-built \wsbook\src\book\j2ee\exchange.ear file into \bea\wlserver6.1\config\mydomain\applications.

Before starting the WebLogic server, edit the \bea\wlserver6.1\config\mydomain\startWebLogic.cmd file and set the STARTMODE flag to `false`. This instructs WebLogic to run in development mode and automatically load .ear files from the mydomain/applications directory.

Then start a WebLogic server, which runs on port 7001 by default and loads any .ear files you have in the /applications directory associated with your domain. Because the build.xml files copied the exchange.ear file into the /mydomain/applications directory, the currency exchange EJB is automatically loaded and its associated StatelessBeanAdapter exposes the EJB as a web service.

You can check that everything is working by launching the WebLogic console and expanding the Deployments/Applications menu (see Figure 7.1).

The build process automatically generates an index.html home page for web services, which in this case has the URL http://localhost:7001/exchange/index.html. If you enter this URL into your browser, you will see a screen like that in Figure 7.2.

To see the home page for the web service, click the link for exchangeService.ExchangeHome (see Figure 7.3).

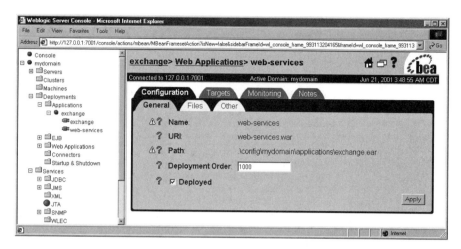

FIGURE 7.1
Checking that all is in order

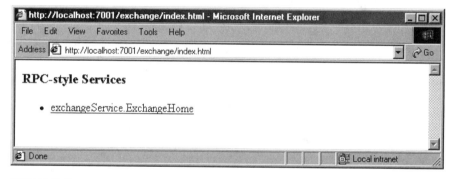

FIGURE 7.2
An index.html home page

FIGURE 7.3
The web service home page

To see the WSDL that was statically generated during the build process, click the WSDL link. As you can see, the WSDL is in the standard format required by SOAP clients (see Figure 7.4).

FIGURE 7.4
The WSDL

For completeness, here is the WSDL file in its entirety.

http://localhost:7001/exchange/
exchangeService.ExchangeHome/wsdl.jsp

```xml
<?xml version="1.0"?>
<definitions
targetNamespace="java:book.j2ee"
  xmlns="http://schemas.xmlsoap.org/wsdl/"
  xmlns:xsi="http://www.w3.org/1999/XMLSchema-instance"
  xmlns:tns="java:book.j2ee"
  xmlns:xsd="http://www.w3.org/1999/XMLSchema"
  xmlns:soap="http://schemas.xmlsoap.org/wsdl/soap/">
  <types>
    <schema
      targetNamespace='java:book.j2ee'
      xmlns='http://www.w3.org/1999/XMLSchema'>
    </schema>
  </types>
  <message name="getValueRequest">
    <part name="arg0" type="xsd:string" />
  </message>
  <message name="getValueResponse">
    <part name="return" type="xsd:double" />
  </message>
  <message name="getRateRequest">
    <part name="arg0" type="xsd:string" />
    <part name="arg1" type="xsd:string" />
  </message>
  <message name="getRateResponse">
    <part name="return" type="xsd:double" />
  </message>
  <message name="setValueRequest">
    <part name="arg0" type="xsd:string" />
    <part name="arg1" type="xsd:double" />
  </message>
  <message name="setValueResponse">
  </message>
  <portType name="IExchangeBeanPortType">
    <operation name="getValue">
      <input message="tns:getValueRequest"/>
      <output message="tns:getValueResponse"/>
    </operation>
    <operation name="setValue">
      <input message="tns:setValueRequest"/>
      <output message="tns:setValueResponse"/>
    </operation>
    <operation name="getRate">
      <input message="tns:getRateRequest"/>
      <output message="tns:getRateResponse"/>
    </operation>
  </portType>
  <binding
    name="IExchangeBeanBinding"
```

```
    type="tns:IExchangeBeanPortType">
    <soap:binding
      style="rpc"
      transport="http://schemas.xmlsoap.org/soap/http/"/>
    <operation name="getValue">
      <soap:operation soapAction="urn:getValue"/>
      <input>
        <soap:body
          use="encoded"
          namespace='urn:IExchangeBean'
          encodingStyle="http://schemas.xmlsoap.org/soap/encoding/"/>
      </input>
      <output>
        <soap:body
          use="encoded"
          namespace='urn:IExchangeBean'
          encodingStyle="http://schemas.xmlsoap.org/soap/encoding/"/>
      </output>
    </operation>
    <operation name="getRate">
      <soap:operation soapAction="urn:getRate"/>
      <input>
        <soap:body
          use="encoded"
          namespace='urn:IExchangeBean'
          encodingStyle="http://schemas.xmlsoap.org/soap/encoding/"/>
      </input>
      <output>
        <soap:body
          use="encoded"
          namespace='urn:IExchangeBean'
          encodingStyle="http://schemas.xmlsoap.org/soap/encoding/"/>
      </output>
    </operation>
    <operation name="setValue">
      <soap:operation
        soapAction="urn:setValue"/>
      <input>
        <soap:body
          use="encoded"
          namespace='urn:IExchangeBean'
          encodingStyle="http://schemas.xmlsoap.org/soap/encoding/"/>
      </input>
      <output>
        <soap:body
          use="encoded"
          namespace='urn:IExchangeBean'
          encodingStyle="http://schemas.xmlsoap.org/soap/encoding/"/>
      </output>
    </operation>
  </binding>
  <service name="IExchangeBean">
    <documentation>todo</documentation>
    <port
      name="IExchangeBeanPort"
```

```
        binding="tns:IExchangeBeanBinding">
        <soap:address location="http://localhost:7001/exchange/
exchangeuri"/>
    </port>
  </service>
</definitions>
```

Now that the EJB is published as a web service, let's try to invoke it from a SOAP client.

Consuming J2EE Web Services

You can bind to and invoke an EJB web service from any SOAP client, such as Apache SOAP, Microsoft .NET, and GLUE.

To invoke the currency exchange EJB web service from GLUE, first create client-side bindings by using the wsdl2java command from the wsbook\src\book\j2ee directory (note that the first two lines are wrapped and should be entered without any break).

```
> wsdl2java http://localhost:7001/exchange/
exchangeService.ExchangeHome/wsdl.jsp
write file IIExchangeBean.java
write file IExchangeBeanHelper.java
> _
```

The IIExchangeBean.java interface that is generated corresponds to the public methods on the EJB exchange web service.

wsbook\src\book\j2ee\IIExchangeBean.java

```
// generated by GLUE

package book.j2ee;

public interface IIExchangeBean
  {
  double getValue( String arg0 );
  double getRate( String arg0, String arg1 );
  void setValue( String arg0, double arg1 );
  }
```

The J2EEClient1 program binds to the EJB web service using the IExchange-BeanHelper class and invokes the getRate() method.

wsbook\src\book\j2ee\J2EEClient1.java

```
package book.j2ee;

import electric.registry.Registry;

public class J2EEClient1
  {
  public static void main( String[] args )
    throws Exception
    {
    // bind to J2EE web service
    IIExchangeBean exchange = IExchangeBeanHelper.bind();

    // invoke the web service as if it was a local java object
    double rate = exchange.getRate( "usa", "japan" );
    System.out.println( "usa/japan exchange rate = " + rate );
    }
  }
```

Here is the output:

```
> java book.j2ee.J2EEClient1
usa/japan exchange rate = 2.5

>
```

Consuming Web Services from J2EE

If you go to the exchange web service home page and click the client.jar link, you can download a client.jar file that contains everything you need to invoke the service from a Java J2EE client with no previously installed SOAP capabilities. The .jar file includes a small SOAP processor and XML parser.

The following example uses client.jar instead of GLUE to bind to and invoke the EJB web service. Make sure that you put the client.jar into your CLASS-PATH before attempting to execute the example.

wsbook\src\book\j2ee\J2EEClient2.java

```
package book.j2ee;

import java.util.Properties;
import javax.naming.Context;
import javax.naming.InitialContext;

public class J2EEClient2
  {
  public static void main( String[] arg )
    throws Exception
    {
    Properties properties = new Properties();
    String contextFactory =
"weblogic.soap.http.SoapInitialContextFactory";
    properties.put( Context.INITIAL_CONTEXT_FACTORY, contextFactory
);
    String interfaceProperty = "weblogic.soap.wsdl.interface";
    properties.put( interfaceProperty, IExchangeBean.class.getName() );
    Context context = new InitialContext( properties );

    // bind to J2EE web service using JNDI
    String url = "http://localhost:7001/exchange/
exchangeService.ExchangeHome/wsdl.jsp;
    IExchangeBean exchange = (IExchangeBean) context.lookup( url );

    // invoke the web service as if it was a local java object
    double rate = exchange.getRate( "usa", "japan" );
    System.out.println( "usa/japan exchange rate = " + rate );
    }
  }
```

Here is the output:

```
> java book.j2ee.J2EEClient2
usa/japan exchange rate = 2.5

>
```

You can use the same client.jar file to bind to any other web service that implements the same interface. To see this, first run the book.soap.ExchangeServer program from earlier in the book to publish an Exchange web service on port 8004. Then run the following client program that uses the client.jar file to bind to the service and invoke it.

wsbook\src\book\j2ee\J2EEClient3.java

```
package book.j2ee;

import java.util.Properties;
import javax.naming.Context;
import javax.naming.InitialContext;

public class J2EEClient3
  {
  public static void main( String[] arg )
    throws Exception
    {
    Properties properties = new Properties();
    String contextFactory =
"weblogic.soap.http.SoapInitialContextFactory";
    properties.put( Context.INITIAL_CONTEXT_FACTORY, contextFactory
);
    String interfaceProperty = "weblogic.soap.wsdl.interface";
    properties.put( interfaceProperty, IExchangeBean.class.getName() );
    Context context = new InitialContext( properties );

    // bind to GLUE web service using JNDI
    String url = "http://localhost:8004/soap/exchange.wsdl";
    IExchangeBean exchange = (IExchangeBean) context.lookup( url );

    // invoke the web service as if it was a local java object
    double rate = exchange.getRate( "usa", "japan" );
    System.out.println( "usa/japan exchange rate = " + rate );
    }
  }
```

Here is the output:

```
> java book.j2ee.J2EEClient3
usa/japan exchange rate = 2.5

>
```

Summary

In this chapter, we saw how an EJB can be published as a web service using the J2EE platform. We demonstrated interoperability by invoking a J2EE web service from GLUE and invoking a GLUE web service using a J2EE client.

In the next chapter, we'll see how the Microsoft .NET platform provides similar support for web services.

Quiz

- What changes must you make to an EJB to make it available as a web service?
- What companies sell J2EE platforms that support web services?

Exercises

1. Discuss whether J2EE should drop RMI and IIOP in favor of SOAP as its primary protocol.
2. How could you support stateful session beans as web services?

.NET Web Services

8

.NET is Microsoft's next-generation technology platform. This chapter shows how .NET supports the development and deployment of web services, and how .NET clients can invoke web services deployed on other platforms.

Overview

.NET, Microsoft's comprehensive platform for next-generation computing, includes rich support for for XML web services.

The key technologies that make up .NET are:

- *CLR (Common Language Runtime)*, which allows most languages to be compiled into a common intermediate language (IL) that is then converted into machine code before execution. Because IL looks the same regardless of which language was used to generate it, CLR allows components written in any language to be mixed-and-matched within the same application. CLR also includes an execution environment with garbage collection, class loading, security, and a just-in-time (JIT) compiler. Visual Studio .NET includes CLR support for Visual Basic, C++, and Microsoft's new language, C# (C sharp).

- *.NET framework*, which is a comprehensive set of reusable components that can be used by any CLR-supported language. The framework includes support for collections, data access, graphics, I/O, messaging, networking, remote method invocation (RMI), security, processes, threads, XML, user interfaces, and much more.

- *ASP.NET*, which is the new-and-improved version of Active Server Pages (ASP) that includes built-in support for web services.

.NET is currently in beta and available only on Windows platforms, although there are some indications that it may become available on other operating systems.

The rest of this chapter shows how web services can be published and consumed using .NET.

Installing .NET

This chapter was written using .NET beta 2, a free evaluation download from http://www.microsoft.com. Although by now there may have been a new release, I don't think future changes will be significant. .NET beta 2 comes on 4 CDs that install the CLR, ASP.NET, and Visual Studio .NET onto your computer. I found the installation process to be very straightforward. To run the examples, make sure that the IIS web server is installed and running.

Publishing .NET Web Services

This section covers the steps necessary to create and publish a .NET web service. The examples are written in C#, which is similar to Java and easy to learn. A similar approach can be used to create .NET web services in any CLR-supported language.

Because you're already familiar with the currency exchange service, let's see what it takes to built a C# web service with the same functionality. When you launch Visual Studio .NET, you're greeted with a start screen (see Figure 8.1) that prompts you to select a project.

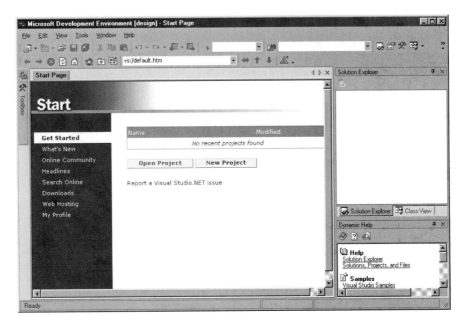

FIGURE 8.1
The Visual Studio .NET start page

To create a C# web service, click New Project and select the ASP.NET Web Service template from the C# project types. In this example (see Figure 8.2), I named the project Currency.

At this point, the Solution Explorer appears with a list of resources that make up the project, together with a blank form associated with the default web service, initially called Service1.asmx (see Figure 8.3).

To enter source code for the service, click the link "click here to switch to code view." The source code view is initialized with a simple web service called Service1 that does nothing (see Figure 8.4).

To change the code into a currency exchange web service:

1. Rename the class to "Exchange".
2. Remove the unnecessary constructor and component designer generated code.
3. Rename Service1.asmx to "Exchange.asmx".
4. Insert `[WebService(Namespace=http://`
   `www.themindelectric.com/example)]` before the class definition to place the exchange service into the specified namespace.

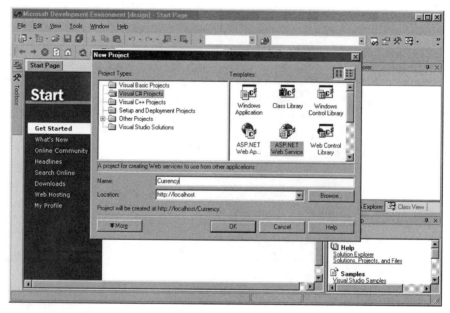

FIGURE 8.2
Creating a C# web service

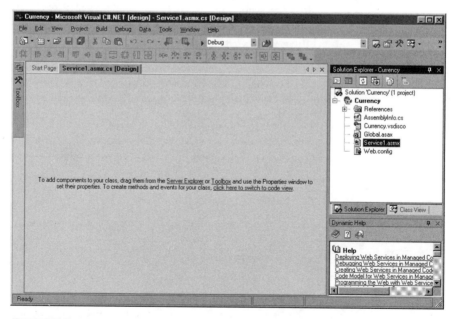

FIGURE 8.3
The Solution Explorer

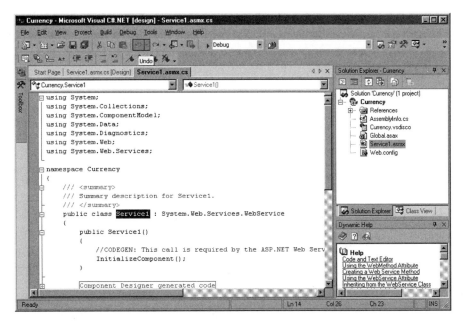

FIGURE 8.4
The Service1 web service

5. Add using   System.Web.Services.Protocols and insert [SoapRpcService()] before the class definition so that requests and responses to this web service use the standard SOAP "section 5" encoding scheme.

6. Replace the dummy method with the code for getRate().

7. Insert [WebMethod] before the getRate() definition to make this method visible to web service clients.

8. Remove the unnecessary using statements at the top of the code.

If you leave off the [SoapRpcService()] attribute, a .NET web service will use literal encoding, which doesn't support cyclic references or special encoding for arrays. Some platforms like GLUE support this encoding style as well, but for maximum portability, it's best to stick with RPC-style encoding.

Here is the source code after these modifications are made. Copies of the .NET examples are included in the wsbook\src\book\net directory.

wsbook\src\book\net\Exchange.asmx.cs

```
using System;
using System.Web.Services;
using System.Web.Services.Protocols;

namespace Currency
  {
  [WebService(Namespace="http://www.themindelectric.com/example")]
  [SoapRpcService()]
  public class Exchange : System.Web.Services.WebService
    {
    [WebMethod]
    public double getRate( String country, String country2 )
      {
      return 122.69; // hard code for demo purposes
      }
    }
  }
```

Behind the scenes, Visual Studio .NET places project files under \Inet-pub\wwwroot\<Name-of-Project>, where \Inetpub\wwwroot is the document base of your local web server. In this case, the \Inetpub\wwwroot\Currency directory is populated with the source code of your project (Exchange.asmx.cs) together with various configuration files, and \Inetpub\wwwroot\Currency\bin contains the compiled versions of the project, together with debugging information.

```
Inetpub
  \wwwroot
    \Currency   (Exchange.asmx, Exchange.asmx.cs, Global.asax,
Web.config)
      \bin (Currency.dll, Current.pdb)
```

The Exchange.asmx file contains a description of the currency exchange web service, including the location of its source code.

Exchange.asmx

```
<%@ WebService Language="c#" Codebehind="Exchange.asmx.cs"
Class="Currency.Exchange" %>
```

The Global.asax file contains a description of the application, including the location of its source code.

Global.asax

```
<%@ Application Codebehind="Global.asax.cs"
Inherits="Currency.Global" %>
```

Because the local .NET web server has its document base set to \Inet-pub\wwwroot, HTTP messages sent to http://localhost/Currency/Exchange.asmx are delivered to the web service described by Exchange.asmx. The web service is automatically activated if it is not already running.

To build and run the web service, press the F5 key. The web service home page is automatically displayed (see Figure 8.5).

If you click the name of an operation, you are presented with a page (see Figure 8.6) that allows you to enter parameters and invoke the web service, which is handy for testing purposes. In addition, the page includes a sample SOAP request and response.

When I entered the arguments usa and japan and pressed Invoke, a new browser popped open with the result (see Figure 8.7).

Note from the browser address window that the web service method was not invoked using SOAP, but with an alternative WSDL binding that allows web services to be invoked by GET/POST messages using the syntax URI/method?arg1=value&arg2=value. Several web services platforms, including .NET and GLUE, support this alternative and complementary form of method invocation.

To see the WSDL for the Exchange service, go back to the web service home page and click the Service Description link. Figure 8.8 shows what you should see.

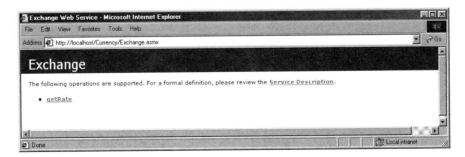

FIGURE 8.5

The web server home page

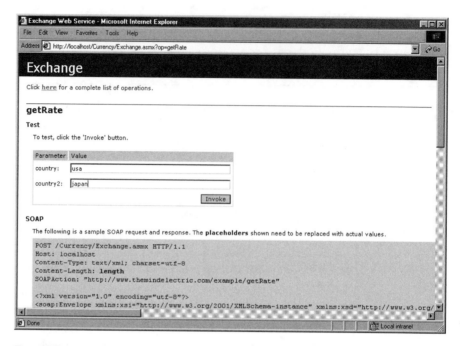

FIGURE 8.6
A page for testing

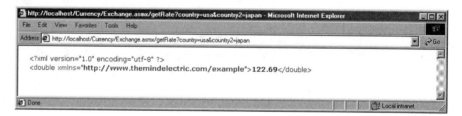

FIGURE 8.7
A new browser

FIGURE 8.8
The WSDL for the Exchange service

Note that the browser points to http://localhost/Currency/ Exchange.asmx?WSDL. In general, placing ?WSDL after the address of a .NET web service causes the WSDL of the web service to be returned.

To create a stripped-down version of the project (see Figure 8.9), click Project/Copy Project, select File Share, and click Only files needed to run this application.

When I followed these steps and renamed the copy MyCurrency, I obtained the following minimal directory structure:

```
Inetpub
  \wwwroot
    \MyCurrency (Exchange.asmx, Global.asax, Web.config)
      \bin (Currency.dll)
```

The web service at this location could then be accessed using http://local-host/MyCurrency.

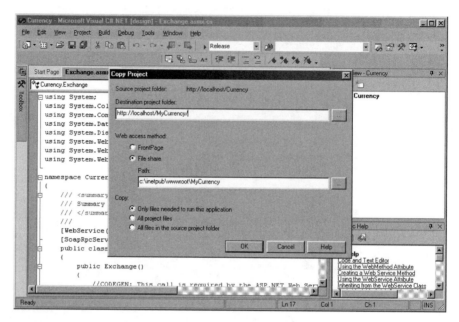

FIGURE 8.9
A stripped-down version

Consuming .NET Web Services

To illustrate the cross-platform nature of web services, let's invoke the .NET currency exchange service from a GLUE client and a J2EE client.

To access the .NET service from GLUE, first type the following `wsdl2java` command from the wsbook\src\book\net directory to generate Java client-side bindings.

```
> wsdl2java http://localhost/Currency/Exchange.asmx?WSDL -p book.net
write file IExchange.java
write file ExchangeHelper.java
> _
```

The `IExchange` interface corresponds to the public methods on the .NET exchange web service.

wsbook\src\book\net\IExchange.java

```
// generated by GLUE
package book.net;

public interface IExchange
  {
  double getRate( String country, String country2 );
  }
```

The NETClient1 programs binds to the .NET web service using the ExchangeHelper class and invokes the getRate() method.

wsbook\src\book\net\NETClient1.java

```
package book.net;

import electric.registry.Registry;

public class NETClient1
  {
  public static void main( String[] args )
    throws Exception
    {
    // bind to .NET web service
    IExchange exchange = ExchangeHelper.bind();

    // invoke the web service as if it was a local java object
    double rate = exchange.getRate( "usa", "japan" );
    System.out.println( "usa/japan exchange rate = " + rate );
    }
  }
```

Here is the output from this program:

```
> java book.net.NETClient1
usa/japan exchange rate = 122.69

> _
```

To access the .NET web service from J2EE, we'll use a variation of the J2EEClient2 program from the previous chapter.

wsbook\src\book\net\NETClient2.java

```
package book.net;

import java.util.Properties;
import javax.naming.Context;
import javax.naming.InitialContext;
import book.j2ee.IExchangeBean;

public class NETClient2
    {
    public static void main( String[] arg )
        throws Exception
        {
        // create J2EE context for Exchange web service
        Properties properties = new Properties();
        String contextFactory =
"weblogic.soap.http.SoapInitialContextFactory";
        properties.put( Context.INITIAL_CONTEXT_FACTORY, contextFactory );
        String interfaceProperty = "weblogic.soap.wsdl.interface";
        properties.put( interfaceProperty, IExchangeBean.class.getName() );
        Context context = new InitialContext( properties );

        // bind to .NET web service using JNDI
        String url = "http://localhost/Currency/Exchange.asmx?WSDL";
        IExchangeBean exchange = (IExchangeBean) context.lookup( url );

        // invoke the web service as if it was a local java object
        double rate = exchange.getRate( "usa", "japan" );
        System.out.println( "usa/japan exchange rate = " + rate );
        }
    }
```

Here is the output from this program:

```
> java book.net.NETClient2
usa/japan exchange rate = 122.69

> _
```

As you can see, it's easy to invoke a .NET web service from a variety of clients, which attests to the rapid adoption of web services technology.

Consuming Web Services from .NET

Visual Studio .NET has a feature called Web References that makes it simple to consume third-party web services. To demonstrate this feature, let's create a C# console application called NETClient that invokes the Exchange web service that was built earlier in this chapter.

Start by selecting New Project, then Console Application, then enter NET-Client as the name of the application (see Figure 8.10).

When you create a console application, you're presented with a blank program that contains a class that does nothing. To use a web service within this application, click Project/Add Web Reference. You are presented with a form that prompts you for the URL of the WSDL for the web service.

In this case, I entered http://localhost/Currency/Exchange.asmx?WSDL, the URL of the .NET web service we created earlier in this chapter.

After a short while, I saw the WSDL displayed in the left window and a synopsis of the web service appear in the right window (see Figure 8.11). To include a reference to this service into your application, simply press Add Reference.

When you do this, Visual Studio .NET automatically creates a local proxy class that represents the remote web service and displays it in your Class view window. Messages sent to an instance of this proxy are automatically

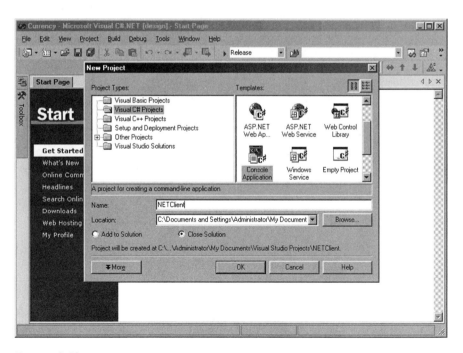

FIGURE 8.10
A C# console application

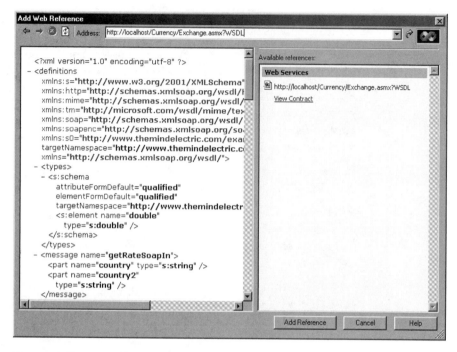

FIGURE 8.11
The WSDL (left) and web service synopses

forwarded to the web service. Because in this case the web service is hosted locally, the namespace of the proxy class is localhost.

To see the web service in action, write a small program that constructs an instance of the proxy class (see Figure 8.12), send it the getRate() message, and then display the result. To prevent the console application from immediately closing, add a Console.ReadLine() statement.

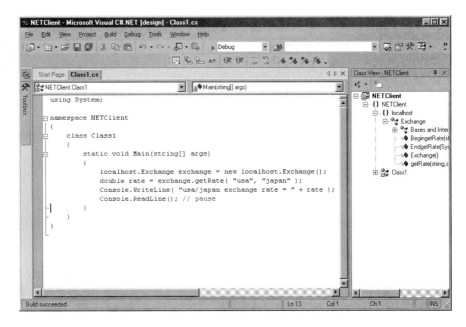

FIGURE 8.12
A proxy class instance

Here is the source code for the .NET client of the .NET web service.

wsbook\src\book\net\Class1.cs

```
using System;

namespace NETClient
  {
  class Class1
    {
    static void Main( string[] args )
      {
      localhost.Exchange exchange = new localhost.Exchange();
      double rate = exchange.getRate( "usa", "japan" );
      Console.WriteLine( "usa/japan exchange rate = " + rate );
      Console.ReadLine(); // pause
      }
    }
  }
```

To run the program, press F5. Figure 8.13 is what you should see:

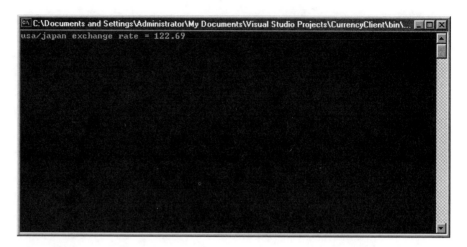

FIGURE 8.13
The web service in action

Note that you do not have to manually start the web service that was built in the last section. The .NET web server detects that you're trying to reach it and automatically loads it into memory

By default, Visual Studio .NET saves your projects under your \Documents and Settings\<Login-Name>\My Documents\Visual Studio Projects\<Project-Name>\bin\Debug directory, so to run this console application directly from the command line, move into the \Documents and Settings\Administrator\My Documents\Visual Studio Projects\NETClient\bin\Debug directory and type NETClient.

Here is what you should see:

```
> NETClient
usa/japan exchange rate = 122.69

> _
```

Because web services are platform and language neutral, you can use .NET to invoke web services hosted on other platforms. For example, let's take a look at how to invoke a GLUE web service using .NET.

To do this, run the ExchangeServer program from Chapter 2 to publish an instance of Exchange to the address localhost:8004/soap/exchange.wsdl.

```
> java book.soap.ExchangeServer
GLUE 1.2 (c) 2001 The Mind Electric
startup server on http://199.174.18.197:8004/soap
```

Then create a C# console application called GLUEClient and add a web reference with the address of the GLUE web service (see Figure 8.14).

Information about the GLUE web service will appear in the class view window and you can construct a proxy to the GLUE Exchange service in the same manner as the previous section (see Figure 8.15).

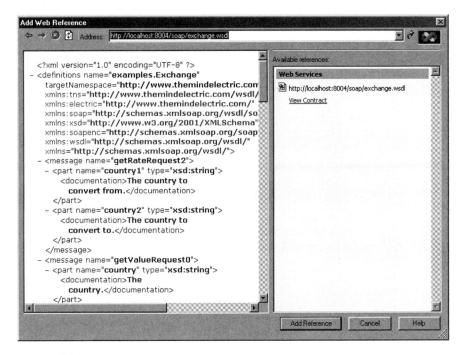

FIGURE 8.14
Invoking a web service

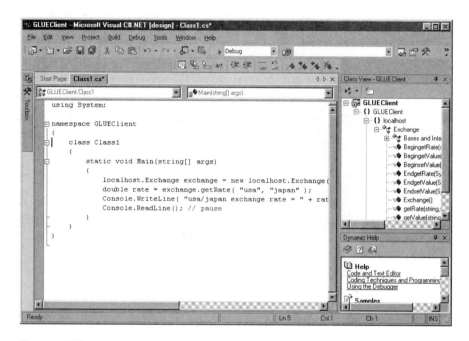

FIGURE 8.15
GLUE web service information

Here is the source code for the .NET client of the GLUE web service.

wsbook\src\book\net\Class2.cs

```
using System;

namespace GLUEClient
  {
  class Class1
    {
    static void Main( string[] args )
      {
      localhost.Exchange exchange = new localhost.Exchange();
      double rate = exchange.getRate( "usa", "japan" );
      Console.WriteLine( "usa/japan exchange rate = " + rate );
      Console.ReadLine(); // pause
      }
    }
  }
```

To run the program, press F5. Figure 8.16 is what you should see:

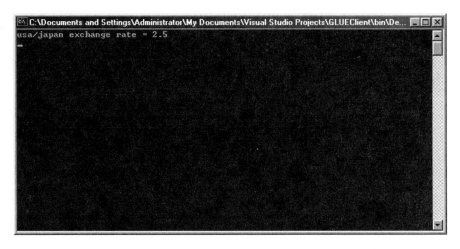

FIGURE 8.16
The final screen

Complex Data Types and .NET

It is fairly straightforward to send complex data types to and from .NET. The Add Web Reference feature of .NET will generate C# data structures for complex data types defined in a WSDL <types> section, and most wsdl2java utilities will generate client-side data structures from .NET WSDL.

Chapter 9 demonstrates how Java objects can be sent and received from .NET.

Summary

In this chapter, we saw how .NET and its companion VisualStudio development environment allow web services to be developed, deployed, and consumed. We also noted that .NET CLR supports multiple languages, including C# which is Microsoft's new preferred language for building .NET applications.

Interoperability was demonstrated first by invoking a .NET web service from GLUE and J2EE, then by invoking a GLUE web service from .NET.

The next chapter presents a more complex example of multiplatform interoperability.

Quiz

- How does .NET allow components written in different languages to be mixed and matched?
- Why is it a good idea to add the `SoapRpcService()` attribute to .NET web services?
- How are .NET web services activated?

Exercises

1. Use Visual Studio to create a Visual Basic version of the currency exchange web service.
2. Compare and contrast the way that J2EE and .NET approach deployment of web services.
3. Create an authenticating .NET web service and access it from GLUE.

Multiplatform Interoperability

9

Now that we've covered SOAP, WSDL, UDDI, and several of the popular platforms for web services, it's time to put it all together. This chapter presents a miniproject that I built from web services hosted by .NET, GLUE, and J2EE, and illustrates how far interoperability has come in just a short time.

Overview

The application that I'll use to demonstrate interoperability is a purchasing service that allows subscribers to purchase items across the Internet using any SOAP client. The purchasing service uses SSL and basic authentication to limit its use to clients that have obtained a user name and password. The application assumes that clients are allocated an account number as part of the subscription process.

The purchasing service has a single operation called purchase that accepts a user's account number and the name of the item to purchase. If the user has

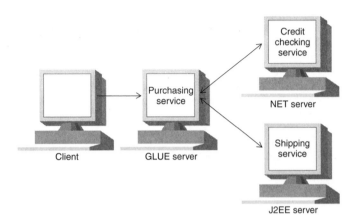

FIGURE 9.1
The purchasing services aggregates credit checking and shipping

good credit, the order is placed and a tracking number for the shipment is returned. If the credit is bad, a credit exception is returned.

The purchasing service uses a credit checking service to perform the credit check, and a shipping service to send the order. The credit checking service is written in C# and hosted in .NET, the shipping service is written in Java and hosted in J2EE, and the purchasing service is written in Java and hosted in GLUE.

The diagram in Figure 9.1 shows how it all fits together.

The rest of this chapter describes how to build each of the web services, how to invoke the purchasing service from a SOAP client, and how UDDI could be used to advertise the purchasing service to the rest of the world.

The .NET Credit Check Service _____

The .NET credit check service is a C# class called CreditCheck that implements a single method called creditCheck that returns a credit report for a specific financial transaction. The transaction is represented by a Transaction object that contains the account number and amount. The credit report is represented by a Report object that contains a boolean which indicates success and a string which indicates the status.

For demonstration purposes, the creditCheck() method is hardcoded with its verification logic. In a real system, the method would consult a database to perform the check.

To create the .NET credit check web service, open a new ASP.NET web service project called CreditCheck and add a C# CreditCheck class with the following source:

wsbook\src\book\interop\net\CreditCheck.asmx.cs

```
using System;
using System.Web;
using System.Web.Services;
using System.Web.Services.Protocols;

namespace MultiPlatformDemo
{
   [WebService(Namespace="http://www.themindelectric.com/example")]
   [SoapRpcService()]
   public class CreditCheck : System.Web.Services.WebService
   {
     [WebMethod]
     public Report checkCredit( Transaction transaction )
     {
       Report report = new Report();

       // hard code logic for demo
       if( transaction.account == 13357 ||
       transaction.amount > 100000 )
       {
       report.ok = false;
       report.status = "not enough funds";
       }
       else
       {
         report.ok = true;
         report.status = "credit is good";
       }

       return report;
     }
   }

   public class Transaction
   {
     public int account;
     public int amount;
   }

   public class Report
   {
     public bool ok;
     public String status;
   }
}
```

Figure 9.2 is a screen shot that shows what the project should look like.
To run the web service, press F5. Figure 9.3 shows what you should see.

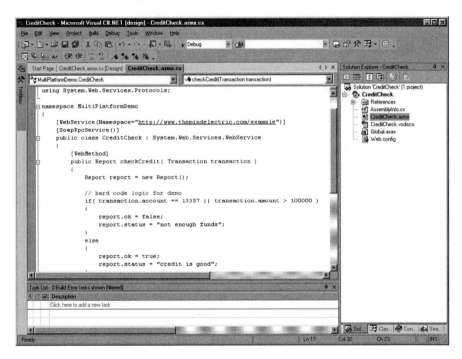

FIGURE 9.2
The CreditCheck demo screen

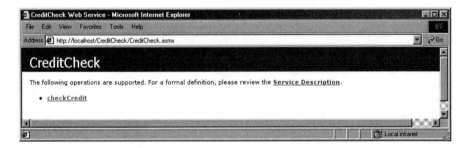

FIGURE 9.3
The CreditCheck web service

Click the creditCheck link to see a detailed description of what a SOAP invocation of the method looks like (see Figure 9.4). Note that the format of a Transaction on the wire matches the format that was described in Chapter 4.

Then go back to the web service home page and click the service description link to see WSDL for the credit check service (see Figure 9.5). Note that the `<types>` section includes schema definitions for the Transaction and Report complex data types.

At this point, the .NET credit service is complete, and ready to be invoked by the purchasing service.

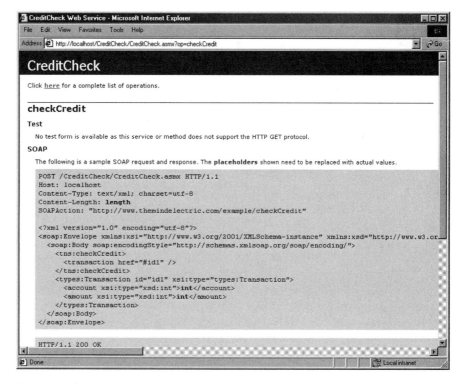

FIGURE 9.4
The SOAP invocation of CreditCheck

FIGURE 9.5
The WSDL for the credit check service

The J2EE Shipping Service

The J2EE shipping service is a stateless session bean called ShippingBean that implements a single send method that returns a tracking number for the requested shipment.

Here is the Shipping interface that defines the send() method.

wsbook\src\book\interop\j2ee\Shipping.java

```java
package book.interop.j2ee;

import java.rmi.RemoteException;
import javax.ejb.EJBObject;

public interface Shipping extends EJBObject
  {
  /**
```

```
   * @param account The user's account number.
   * @param item The item to send
   * @throws RemoteException If a communication error occurs.
   * @return A tracking number for the shipment.
   */
 int send( int account, String item ) throws RemoteException;
 }
```

The ShippingBean stateless session bean implements send(), and for the purposes of this demonstration returns a random positive integer as the tracking number. In a real system, the shipment request would look up the user's address from a database using the account number as the key, create a database record corresponding to the shipment, and return a tracking number that is the key to the shipment record.

Here is the code for the ShippingBean.

wsbook\src\book\interop\j2ee\ShippingBean.java

```
package book.interop.j2ee;

import java.util.*;
import javax.ejb.CreateException;
import javax.ejb.SessionBean;
import javax.ejb.SessionContext;
import javax.naming.InitialContext;
import javax.naming.NamingException;

public class ShippingBean implements SessionBean
   {
   static Random random = new Random();

   // STANDARD EJB STATELESS SESSION BEAN METHODS

   public void setSessionContext( SessionContext context )
      {
      }

   public void ejbActivate()
      {
      }

   public void ejbRemove()
      {
      }

   public void ejbPassivate()
      {
      }
```

```
public void ejbCreate ()
  throws CreateException
  {
  try
    {
    InitialContext initialContext = new InitialContext();
    }
  catch( NamingException exception )
    {
    throw new CreateException( "failed to find environment value "
+ exception );
    }
  }

// DOMAIN-SPECIFIC METHODS

/**
  * @param account The user's account number.
  * @param item The item to send
  * @return A tracking number for the shipment.
  */
public int send( int account, String item )
  {
  return Math.abs( random.nextInt() ); // return random number for
demo
  }
}
```

The ShippingHome home interface is straightforward.

wsbook\src\book\interop\j2ee\ShippingHome.java

```
package book.interop.j2ee;

import java.rmi.RemoteException;
import javax.ejb.CreateException;
import javax.ejb.EJBHome;

public interface ShippingHome extends EJBHome
  {
  Shipping create() throws CreateException, RemoteException;
  }
```

To build the J2EE web service using Ant, the following files are required:

- build.xml—highest level build file
- project.properties—properties used by other build files
- build-ejb.xml—build file specific to EJB
- ejb-jar.xml—standard EJB instructions read by build-ejb.xml

- Weblogic-ejb-jar.xml—WebLogic-specific EJB instructions read by build-ejb.xml
- build-ws.xml—build file that creates the web service specific files code

Here is the high-level build.xml file:

wsbook\src\book\interop\j2ee\build.xml

```
<project name="shipping" default="webservice">
  <target name="webservice">
    <ant dir="." antfile="build-ejb.xml"/>
    <ant dir="." antfile="build-ws.xml"/>
  </target>
</project>
```

The project-properties file defines the WebLogic home and the directory location to place the resulting shipping.ear file.

wsbook\src\book\interop\j2ee\project.properties

```
WL_HOME=C:/bea/wlserver6.1
APPLICATIONS=C:/bea/wlserver6.1/config/mydomain/applications
```

The build-ejb.xml file tells Ant how to build the EJB.

wsbook\src\book\interop\j2ee\build-ejb.xml

```
<project name="ejb-basic-statelessSession" default="all" basedir=".">
  <!-- set global properties for this build -->
  <property file="project.properties"/>
  <property name="src" value="."/>
  <property name="build" value="${src}/build"/>
  <property name="dist" value="."/>
  <property name="WL_HOME" value=""/>

  <target name="all" depends="clean, init, compile_ejb, jar_ejb,
ejbc"/>

  <target name="init">
    <!-- Create the time stamp -->
    <tstamp/>
    <!-- Create the build directory structure used by compile and
copy the deployment descriptors into it-->
    <mkdir dir="${build}"/>
    <mkdir dir="${build}/META-INF"/>
    <copy todir="${build}/META-INF">
      <fileset dir="${src}">
```

```
            <include name="*.xml"/>
         </fileset>
      </copy>
   </target>

   <!-- Compile ejb classes into the build directory (jar preparation)
-->
   <target name="compile_ejb">
      <javac srcdir="${src}" destdir="${build}"
includes="Shipping.java, ShippingHome.java, ShippingBean.java"/>
   </target>

   <!-- Make a standard ejb jar file, including XML deployment
descriptors -->
   <target name="jar_ejb" depends="compile_ejb">
      <jar jarfile="${dist}/a_shipping.jar" basedir="${build}"></jar>
   </target>

   <!-- Run ejbc to create the deployable jar file -->
   <target name="ejbc" depends="jar_ejb">
      <java classname="weblogic.ejbc" fork="yes">
         <sysproperty key="weblogic.home" value="${WL_HOME}"/>
         <arg line="-compiler javac ${dist}/a_shipping.jar ./
shipping.jar"/>
         <classpath>
            <pathelement path="${WL_HOME}/lib/weblogic_sp.jar;${WL_HOME}/
lib/weblogic.jar"/>
         </classpath>
      </java>
   </target>

   <target name="clean">
      <delete dir="${build}"/>
   </target>
</project>
```

The ejb-jar.xml file defines the standard settings for the stateless session bean.

wsbook\src\book\interop\j2ee\ejb-jar.xml

```
<project name="ejb-basic-statelessSession" default="all" basedir=".">
   <!-- set global properties for this build -->
   <property file="project.properties"/>
   <property name="src" value="."/>
   <property name="build" value="${src}/build"/>
   <property name="dist" value="."/>
   <property name="WL_HOME" value=""/>

   <target name="all" depends="clean, init, compile_ejb, jar_ejb, ejbc"/>
```

```
  <target name="init">
    <!-- Create the time stamp -->
    <tstamp/>
    <!-- Create the build directory structure used by compile and
copy the deployment descriptors into it-->
    <mkdir dir="${build}"/>
    <mkdir dir="${build}/META-INF"/>
    <copy todir="${build}/META-INF">
      <fileset dir="${src}">
        <include name="*.xml"/>
      </fileset>
    </copy>
  </target>

  <!-- Compile ejb classes into the build directory (jar preparation)
-->
  <target name="compile_ejb">
    <javac srcdir="${src}" destdir="${build}"
includes="Shipping.java, ShippingHome.java, ShippingBean.java"/>
  </target>

  <!-- Make a standard ejb jar file, including XML deployment
descriptors -->
  <target name="jar_ejb" depends="compile_ejb">
    <jar jarfile="${dist}/a_shipping.jar" basedir="${build}"></jar>
  </target>

  <!-- Run ejbc to create the deployable jar file -->
  <target name="ejbc" depends="jar_ejb">
    <java classname="weblogic.ejbc" fork="yes">
      <sysproperty key="weblogic.home" value="${WL_HOME}"/>
      <arg line="-compiler javac ${dist}/a_shipping.jar ./
shipping.jar"/>
      <classpath>
        <pathelement path="${WL_HOME}/lib/weblogic_sp.jar;${WL_HOME}/
lib/weblogic.jar"/>
      </classpath>
    </java>
  </target>

  <target name="clean">
    <delete dir="${build}"/>
  </target>
</project>
```

The weblogic-ejb-jar.xml file defines the additional WebLogic-specific settings, including the JDNI name for the bean which in this case is shipping-Service.ShippingHome.

wsbook\src\book\interop\j2ee\weblogic-ejb-jar.xml

```
<?xml version="1.0"?>
<!DOCTYPE weblogic-ejb-jar PUBLIC '-//BEA Systems, Inc.//DTD WebLogic
5.1.0 EJB//EN' 'http://www.bea.com/servers/wls510/dtd/weblogic-ejb-
jar.dtd'>
<weblogic-ejb-jar>
  <weblogic-enterprise-bean>
    <ejb-name>shippingService</ejb-name>
    <caching-descriptor>
      <max-beans-in-free-pool>100</max-beans-in-free-pool>
    </caching-descriptor>
    <jndi-name>shippingService.ShippingHome</jndi-name>
  </weblogic-enterprise-bean>
</weblogic-ejb-jar>
```

The final configuration file, build-ws.xml, instructs Ant that the J2EE server will be running on port 7001 with the URI /shippinguri.

wsbook\src\book\interop\j2ee\build-ws.xml

```
<project name="shipping-webservice" default="copy">
  <!-- set global properties for this build -->
  <property file="project.properties"/>
  <property name="module" value="shipping"/>
  <property name="jar.path" value="${module}.jar"/>
  <property name="ear.path" value="${module}.ear"/>

  <target name="wsgen">
    <wsgen destpath="${ear.path}" context="/shipping"
host="localhost" port="7001">
      <rpcservices path="${jar.path}">
        <rpcservice bean="shippingService" uri="/shippinguri"/>
      </rpcservices>
    </wsgen>
  </target>

  <target name="copy" depends="wsgen">
    <copy file="${ear.path}" todir="${APPLICATIONS}"/>
  </target>
</project>
```

To build the EJB web service, type the following command from the wsbook\src\book\interop\j2ee directory.

```
> bea\wlserver6.1\bin\ant
Buildfile: build.xml
```

```
webservice:

clean:

init:
  [mkdir] Created dir: C:\book\src\book\interop\j2ee\build
  [mkdir] Created dir: C:\book\src\book\interop\j2ee\build\META-INF
  [copy] Copying 5 files to C:\book\src\book\interop\j2ee\build\META-
INF

compile_ejb:
  [javac] Compiling 3 source files to
C:\book\src\book\interop\j2ee\build

jar_ejb:
  [jar] Building jar: C:\book\src\book\interop\j2ee\a_shipping.jar

ejbc:

all:

wsgen:

copy:
  [copy] Copying 1 file to
C:\bea\wlserver6.1\config\mydomain\applications

BUILD SUCCESSFUL

Total time: 38 seconds

> _
```

The build process creates an Enterprise Application Resource file called shipping.ear and copies it into the \bea\wlserver6.1\config\mydomain\applications directory.

If you wish to skip the build process for now, simply copy the pre-built \wsbook\src\book\interop\j2ee\shipping.ear file into bea\wlserver6.1\config\mydomain\applications.

When you start BEA WebLogic on port 7001, it detects the .ear file in the applications directory and automatically loads it. To see the home page for the shipping web service, enter the URL http://localhost:7001/shipping/index.html into your web browser. Figure 9.6 illustrates what you should see.

Click the hyperlinked JNDI name to see the home page for the shipping service, which looks like the screen shot in Figure 9.7.

FIGURE 9.6
Shipping web service home page

FIGURE 9.7
shippingService home page

Then click on the WSDL link to see the XML description of the J2EE ship-ping web service (see Figure 9.8).

At this point, the shipping service is complete, and ready to be invoked by the purchasing service.

```
http://localhost:7001/shipping/shippingService.ShippingHome/wsdl.jsp - Microsoft Internet Exp...
File   Edit   View   Favorites   Tools   Help
Address  http://localhost:7001/shipping/shippingService.ShippingHome/wsdl.jsp          Go

  <?xml version="1.0" ?>
- <definitions targetNamespace="java:book.interop.j2ee"
    xmlns="http://schemas.xmlsoap.org/wsdl/"
    xmlns:tns="java:book.interop.j2ee"
    xmlns:xsi="http://www.w3.org/1999/XMLSchema-instance"
    xmlns:xsd="http://www.w3.org/1999/XMLSchema"
    xmlns:soap="http://schemas.xmlsoap.org/wsdl/soap/">
  - <types>
      <schema targetNamespace="java:book.interop.j2ee"
        xmlns="http://www.w3.org/1999/XMLSchema" />
    </types>
  - <message name="sendRequest">
      <part name="arg0" type="xsd:int" />
      <part name="arg1" type="xsd:string" />
    </message>
  - <message name="sendResponse">
      <part name="return" type="xsd:int" />
    </message>
  - <portType name="ShippingPortType">
    - <operation name="send">
        <input message="tns:sendRequest" />
        <output message="tns:sendResponse" />
      </operation>
    </portType>
  - <binding name="ShippingBinding" type="tns:ShippingPortType">
      <soap:binding style="rpc"
        transport="http://schemas.xmlsoap.org/soap/http/" />
    - <operation name="send">
        <soap:operation soapAction="urn:send" />
      - <input>
          <soap:body use="encoded" namespace="urn:Shipping"

 Done                                                    Local intranet
```

FIGURE 9.8
The J2EE shipping web service XML description

The GLUE Purchasing Service _____

The purchasing service acts primarily as an aggregator, orchestrating the credit check and shipping services in response to an incoming purchase request.

In this section, we create Java bindings for the .NET web service and the J2EE web service. Then we create a purchasing service that uses these Java binding to aggregate and orchestrate the services.

Creating Java Bindings for the .NET Web Service

Type the following command from the wsbook\src\book\interop\glue directory to created Java bindings for the .NET credit check service.

```
> wsdl2java http://localhost/CreditCheck/CreditCheck.asmx?WSDL
  -p book.interop.glue
write file ICreditCheck.java
write file CreditCheckHelper.java
write file Transaction.java
write file Report.java
write file CreditCheck.map
> _
```

The ICreditCheck interface defines a single method that accepts a Transaction and returns a Report.

wsbook\src\book\interop\glue\ICreditCheck.java

```
// generated by GLUE
package book.interop.glue;

public interface ICreditCheck
   {
   Report checkCredit( Transaction transaction );
   }
```

The Transaction and Report classes are simple data structures generated from their corresponding .NET WSDL schema definitions.

wsbook\src\book\interop\glue\Transaction.java

```
// generated by GLUE
package book.interop.glue;

public class Transaction
   {
   public int account;
   public int amount;
   }
```

wsbook\src\book\interop\glue\Report.java

```
// generated by GLUE
package book.interop.glue;

public class Report
  {
  public boolean ok;
  public String status;
  }
```

CreditCheck.map contains annotated schemas that define the Java to XML mappings. The annotations are shown bolded for clarity.

wsbook\src\book\interop\glue\CreditCheck.map

```
<?xml version='1.0' encoding='UTF-8'?>
<!--generated by GLUE-->
<mappings xmlns='http://www.themindelectric.com/schema/'>
  <schema xmlns='http://www.w3.org/2001/XMLSchema'
targetNamespace='http://www.themindelectric.com/example/encodedTypes'
xmlns:electric='http://www.themindelectric.com/schema/'>
    <complexType name='Transaction'
electric:class='book.interop.glue.Transaction'>
      <sequence>
        <element name='account' electric:field='account' type='int'/>
        <element name='amount' electric:field='amount' type='int'/>
      </sequence>
    </complexType>
  </schema>
  <schema xmlns='http://www.w3.org/2001/XMLSchema'
targetNamespace='http://www.themindelectric.com/example/encodedTypes'
xmlns:electric='http://www.themindelectric.com/schema/'>
    <complexType name='Report'
electric:class='book.interop.glue.Report'>
      <sequence>
        <element name='ok' electric:field='ok' type='boolean'/>
        <element name='status' electric:field='status' type='string'/
>
      </sequence>
    </complexType>
  </schema>
</mappings>
```

Creating Bindings for the J2EE Web Service

Type the following command from the wsbook\src\book\interop\glue directory to created Java bindings for the J2EE shipping service.

```
> wsdl2java http://localhost:7001/shipping/shippingService.Shi
  ppingHome/wsdl.jsp -p book.interop.glue
write file IShipping.java
write file ShippingHelper.java
> _
```

The IShipping interface defines a single method that accepts an account number and item, and returns a tracking number. The method arguments are called arg0 and arg1 because BEA WebLogic does not extract argument names from Java code.

wsbook\src\book\interop\glue\IShipping.java

```
// generated by GLUE
package book.interop.glue;

public interface IShipping
  {
  int send( int arg0, String arg1 );
  }
```

Creating the Purchasing Web Service

The purchasing service implements the following interface.

wsbook\src\book\interop\glue\IPurchasing.java

```
package book.interop.glue;

public interface IPurchasing
  {
  /**
   * Purchase the specified item, debiting the user's account,
   * and return a shipping tracking number for the order.
   * @param account The user's account number.
   * @param item The item to purchase
   * @throws CreditException If the user's credit is not OK.
   * @return The shipping tracking number.
   */
  int purchase( int account, String item ) throws CreditException;
  }
```

The Purchasing class implements `IPurchasing` and orchestrates a credit check service and a shipping service via the `ICreditCheck` and `IShipping` interfaces, respectively. Notice that the implementation does not contain any code specific to web services.

wsbook\src\book\interop\glue\Purchasing.java

```
package book.interop.glue;

public class Purchasing implements IPurchasing
  {
  IShipping shipping;
  ICreditCheck creditCheck;

  /**
   * @param shipping The shipping service to use.
   * @param creditCheck The credit service to use.
   */
  public Purchasing( IShipping shipping, ICreditCheck creditCheck )
    {
    this.shipping = shipping;
    this.creditCheck = creditCheck;
    }

  /**
   * @param account The user's account number.
   * @param item The item to purchase.
   * @throws CreditException If the user's credit is not OK.
   * @return A tracking number for the item shipment.
   */
  public int purchase( int account, String item ) throws
CreditException
    {
    System.out.println( "purchase( " + account + ", " + item + " )"
);

    // create transaction object, set amount using hardcoded logic
    Transaction transaction = new Transaction();
    transaction.account = account;

    if( item.equals( "shoes" ) )
      transaction.amount = 50;
    else if( item.equals( "socks" ) )
      transaction.amount = 10;
    else
      transaction.amount = 0;

    // call credit check web service, get back Report object
    Report report = creditCheck.checkCredit( transaction );
    System.out.println( "creditCheck( " + account + " ) returns " +
report.ok );
```

```
    // throw exception if the credit was bad
    if( !report.ok )
      throw new CreditException( "bad credit", "<detail><account>" +
report.status + "</account></detail>" );

    // call shipping web service, get back tracking number
    int trackingNumber = shipping.send( account, item );
    System.out.println( "send( " + account + ", " + item + " ) returns "
+ trackingNumber );

    // return tracking number
    return trackingNumber;
    }
  }
```

The PurchasingServer program binds to the credit check and shipping services using the helper classes generated by wsdl2java, and constructs a purchasing service that aggregates them via their proxies. The purchasing service is published on an HTTPS endpoint and a security realm is initialized with information about the authorized clients. See Chapter 5 for more information about publishing secure web services.

wsbook\src\book\interop\glue\PurchasingServer.java

```
package book.interop.glue;

import electric.server.http.HTTP;
import electric.net.http.HTTPContext;
import electric.xml.io.Mappings;
import electric.registry.Registry;
import electric.security.*;

public class PurchasingServer
    {
    public static void main( String[] args )
      throws Exception
      {
      // read java/xml mappings for credit check service
      Mappings.readMappings( "CreditCheck.map" );

      // construct local security realm
      BasicRealm myRealm = new BasicRealm( "myrealm" );

      // add realm to collection of registered realms
      Realms.addRealm( myRealm );

      // principal name="evangelion", password="genesis",
role="subscriber"
      myRealm.addPrincipal( "evangelion", "genesis", new String[]{
"subscriber" } );
```

```
    // start secure web server on port 8004, accept messages via /soap
    HTTPContext context = HTTP.startup( "https://localhost:8004/soap"
);

    // set realm for this context
    context.setRealm( myRealm );

    // bind to shipping service
    System.out.println( "binding to shipping service..." );
    IShipping shipping = ShippingHelper.bind();

    // bind to credit service
    System.out.println( "binding to credit service..." );
    ICreditCheck checkCredit = CreditCheckHelper.bind();

    // create purchasing service
    System.out.println( "publishing purchasing service..." );
    Purchasing purchasing = new Purchasing( shipping, checkCredit );

    // indicate readiness
    System.out.println( "ready." );

    // only allow principals with subscriber role to access
"purchasing"
    context.addGuard( "purchasing", new HasRole( "subscriber" ) );

    // publish purchasing service
    Registry.publish( "purchasing", purchasing );
    }
  }
```

To run the purchasing service, make sure that the J2EE server is running, then run the server program. Here is the server output:

```
> java book.interop.glue.PurchasingServer
GLUE 1.2 (c) 2001 The Mind Electric
startup server on https://199.174.18.241:8004/soap
binding to shipping service...
binding to credit service...
publishing purchasing service...
ready.
```

To see the WSDL for the purchasing service, enter the URL https://localhost:8004/soap/purchasing.wsdl into your browser. You should see the screen in Figure 9.9.

At this point, the secure and authenticating purchasing service is ready to be used.

FIGURE 9.9
The WSDL for the purchasing service

The GLUE Client

This section describes the construction of a client that accesses the purchasing service. It uses GLUE, but could just as well have used .NET, J2EE, or any other SOAP client.

To create client-side Java bindings for the purchasing service, type the following command from the wsbook\src\book\interop\client directory. The -c (checked exceptions) option causes RemoteExceptions to be explicitly thrown in the generated Java interface. The first two lines were entered as a single command.

```
> wsdl2java https://localhost:8004/soap/purchasing.wsdl -c
  -p book.interop.client
write file IPurchasing.java
write file PurchasingHelper.java
> _
```

The IPurchasing interface defines a single method for performing a purchase request.

wsbook\src\book\interop\client\IPurchasing.java

```java
// generated by GLUE
package book.interop.client;

import java.rmi.RemoteException;

public interface IPurchasing
  {
  int purchase( int account, String item ) throws RemoteException;
  }
```

The main client program binds to the purchasing service using credentials (as described in Chapter 5) and invokes the service twice. The second invocation causes the server to throw a CreditException, which is then displayed on the client side.

wsbook\src\book\interop\client\Client.java

```java
package book.interop.client;

import electric.util.Context;
import electric.registry.Registry;
import electric.net.soap.SOAPException;

public class Client
  {
  public static void main( String[] args )
    throws Exception
    {
    try
      {
      // URL of publishing service
      String url = "https://localhost:8004/soap/purchasing.wsdl";

      // bind to the publishing service with credentials
      Context context = new Context();
      context.setProperty( "authUser", "evangelion" );
      context.setProperty( "authPassword", "genesis" );
```

```
        IPurchasing purchasing = (IPurchasing) Registry.bind( url,
IPurchasing.class, context );

        // call the service
        System.out.println( "call purchase( 24456, \"shoes\" )" );
        int trackingNumber1 = purchasing.purchase( 24456, "shoes" );
        System.out.println( "tracking number = " + trackingNumber1 );

        // call the service again
        System.out.println( "call purchase( 13357, \"socks\" )" );
        int trackingNumber2 = purchasing.purchase( 13357, "socks" );
        System.out.println( "tracking number = " + trackingNumber2 );
        }
    catch( SOAPException exception )
        {
        System.out.println( "exception = " + exception );
        System.out.println( "detail =\n" + exception.getSOAPDetail() );
        }
    }
  }
```

To run the client, make sure the J2EE server is running, then type the following command:

```
> java book.interop.client.Client
call purchase( 24456, "shoes" )
tracking number = 1098367385

call purchase( 13357, "socks" )
exception = SOAPException( Server: bad credit )
detail =
<detail>
  <account>not enough funds</account>
</detail>
> _
```

The output from the server, which tracks the progress of the individual service calls as well as the aggregate result, should look like this:

```
> java book.interop.glue.PurchasingServer
GLUE 1.2 (c) 2001 The Mind Electric
startup server on https://199.174.18.241:8004/soap
binding to shipping service...
binding to credit service...
publishing purchasing service...
ready.
purchase( 24456, shoes )
creditCheck( 24456 ) returns true
send( 24456, shoes ) returns 1098367385
purchase( 13357, socks )
creditCheck( 13357 ) returns false
```

The next section describes how UDDI could be used to advertise the purchasing service for use by a broad audience.

Using UDDI

Let's say that you'd like to use UDDI to advertise the purchasing service. If an industry standard TModel for this kind of service does not exist, the first step would be to publish a TModel that describes the service and points to its WSDL interface file (which defines everything about a service except for its endpoint). Once the TModel has been registered, any vendor can publish information about its implementation of the service, such as its endpoint and a brief description.

Then, to locate an implementation of the purchasing service, a client would browse a UDDI registry and search for the service based on keywords or other criteria. When the desired service is located, the client would then note the URL of the WSDL interface file associated with the TModel, and the endpoint of the particular service implementation. The client could then use a tool like wsdl2java to create client-side bindings for the selected service. If necessary, the client would also contact the vendor to obtain a subscription to the service.

Chapter 6 contains more information on how to bind to a service based on its WSDL and endpoint.

Summary

In this chapter, we created a purchasing service by aggregating and orchestrating a .NET credit service and a J2EE shipping service. The purchasing service used SSL and HTTP basic authentication to provide SOAP clients with secure access. The demonstration included an example of passing objects between GLUE and .NET without any need for custom serialization.

The final chapter describes the trend towards decentralized, peer-to-peer computing and a possible future for web services.

Exercises

1. Publish a TModel for the purchasing service to the IBM UDDI repository.

2. Publish an implementation of a purchasing service based on the TModel from (1).

3. Write a client that binds to a purchasing service that implements the TModel from (1).

P2P and the Future of Web Services

I mentioned in the introduction that the final chapter of my last book was dedictated to the future of distributed computing, and that many of the predictions are already coming true. So, in keeping with my tradition, this chapter presents thoughts about what might happen in the field of distributed computing over the next 10 years.

The Trend Toward Decentralization

The primary trend in the world of distributed computing is toward *decentralization*.

In the early days, computers were expensive, bulky, and required special air-conditioned environments. These machines were called *mainframes*, and only large companies could afford them. Access to the systems was typically through paper tape, punched cards, and remote terminals.

Improvements in technology gave rise to *minicomputers* that were still fairly large but could be afforded by smaller businesses and universities. The introduction of the *personal computer* fueled the trend toward smaller and cheaper computing, and brought the benefits of spreadsheets, word processors, and other productivity tools to the masses (see Figure 10.1).

The availability of computer power outside of the traditional glass houses of the corporate computer center caused IT departments some headaches. For example, how do you ensure that the data that is copied from the corporate database to the executive PCs remains secure? And how do the executives know that the data they're looking at on their PCs is up-to-date?

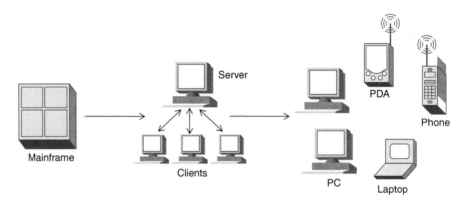

FIGURE 10.1
Computers keep getting smaller and more numerous

Client/Server

One solution is an architecture called client/server that succeeded main-frame computing as the dominant enterprise architecture. With this approach, servers controlled by the IT department host a replicated subset of the mainframe data and provide a set of software services to client computers that typically just run a user interface. This three-tier architecture takes some of the processing burden from the mainframe without losing control of the data to the clients (see Figure 10.2).

The client/server approach works fairly well in corporate settings, but does not scale well for systems that must work on a global scale. For example, if you wanted to implement a music sharing system using a three-tier architecture, the number of servers would be enormous because music sharing systems must replicate multimegabyte digital music files to millions of clients every day.

What is needed is a new kind of computing architecture that takes advantage of the large number of computers without incurring the bottlenecks of a server-centric design.

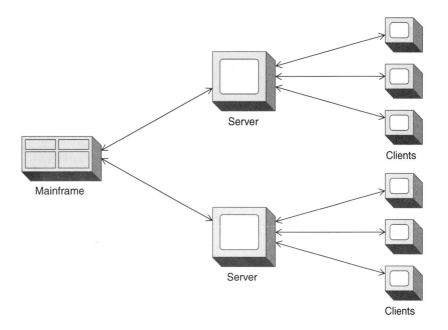

FIGURE 10.2
Three-tier architecture

Peer-to-Peer Computing

Peer-to-peer (P2P) architectures are the most promising approach for the construction of very large-scale distributed systems. The characteristics of P2P architectures are:

- Each node can be both a client and a server.
- A node can disconnect from the network without warning.
- A node is usually an inexpensive device such as a PC or personal digital assistant (PDA).
- There are usually lots of nodes.
- Data and services are often replicated on a large number of nodes.

One of the first high-profile systems built using a form of P2P architecture was called Napster.

Napster

Napster is a music sharing service that allows consumers to swap music files directly between their home computers without storing the music on any central servers. When a client connects to a Napster server in order to share some music files, it uploads a list of the music files on its hard drive to the server. When a client performs a search, the Napster server searches through its database and returns addresses of other clients that have the music. At this point, the client requests the music directly from the other clients and the Napster server is out of the picture (see Figure 10.3).

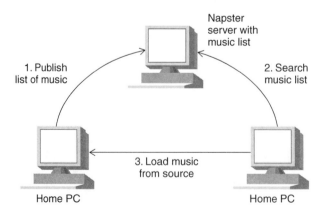

FIGURE 10.3
Napster architecture

Napster is not a pure P2P system because it still relies on a relatively low number of servers to provide the file matching service. Enter Gnutella!

Gnutella

Gnutella is an example of a pure P2P system because it is not run by a single company and has no nodes which act only as servers. Before a computer running Gnutella can share music files, it must connect to a Gnutella network, which is a loose federation of other computers running Gnutella. To connect to a Gnutella network, a computer only has to know the address of one other Gnutella machine on the network, which can usually be obtained from one of several well-known web sites. When a computer connects for the first time, it receives the addresses of hundreds of other machines on the network that it can use when connecting on subsequent occasions. A Gnutella program typically tries to maintain three or four connections to other Gnutella machines at any one time, and regrows connections if an existing connection is broken. A Gnutella network is thus a self-healing, highly inter-connected mesh (see Figure 10.4).

When a Gnutella program wants to find a file, it sends a request to its neighbors with the name of the file to be found, the number of hops so far, and the maximum number of hops. If a neighbor has a matching file, it responds with the location of the file so that the original requestor can load it if

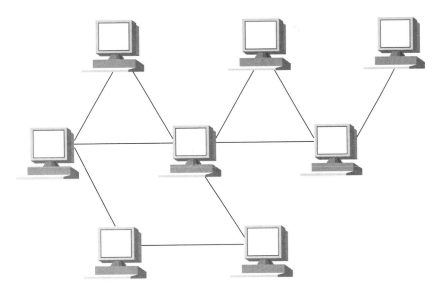

FIGURE 10.4
Gnutella mesh connects peers

desired. In addition, if the maximum number of hops has not been reached, the hop count is incremented and the request is forwarded to all of the neighbor's neighbors. The request rapidly propagates in this manner like a ripple in a pond, effectively searching a good percentage of the network without passing through any kind of centralized server (see Figure 10.5).

The main strength of Gnutella is simplicity, which is also its primary weakness. Because every request is blindly propagated through the mesh, a Gnutella network can quickly saturate, and it is not uncommon for searches to take minutes in order to complete.

FastTrack

A company called FastTrack takes a more sophisticated approach, resulting in much faster search times. The FastTrack architecture allows nodes to morph dynamically into supernodes, which are essentially experts that index the contents of other nodes on the network. When a node sends a request, it is routed to a supernode instead of to all its surrounding neighbors. Nodes typically elect to become supernodes if they have plenty of unused bandwidth and storage, and can choose to revoke their supernode status whenever they wish. A FastTrack network is therefore more adaptive than a Gnutella, and introduces dynamic asymmetries that can be exploited by the search process (see Figure 10.6).

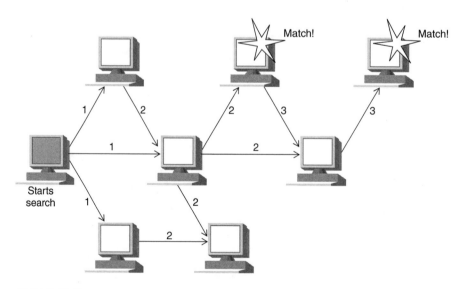

FIGURE 10.5
A Gnutella search fans out like a wave

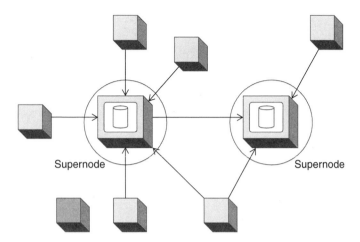

FIGURE 10.6
Supernodes accumulate knowledge about the nodes around them

P2P as General Architecture for Distributed Computing

The main lesson that P2P systems teach is that it is possible to build large-scale, reliable systems from small, cheap, unreliable parts. Several companies are working on general P2P platforms that will allow developers to create applications that take advantage of inexpensive networked computers. The goal is for a program built using a P2P platform to scale from a single machine to a large federation of PCs scattered over the Internet, without modification or significant programmer effort.

JXTA, pioneered by Sun, is one such project that is trying to define a general purpose P2P platform for things like publishing, locating and invoking services in a highly distributed environment.

Even without such a platform, companies like Intel and Sun have been using desktop computers for quite a while to run P2P applications for doing things like integrated circuit design. Intel has estimated that this approach has saved millions of dollars a year that would otherwise have been spent on buying big servers.

Applications for P2P Architectures

Imagine a distributed education system that would allow anyone to upload and share knowledge in a similar way that people can use Napster to share music. This knowledge could be stored in the network cloud as XML and used for purposes such as training materials, quizzes, and online encyclopedias. The amount of processing power and storage that would be necessary for such a system strongly suggests a P2P architecture that could utilize the millions of home computers.

Projects like Microsoft HailStorm aim to provide consumers with a place in the network cloud where they can store things like their calendar, schedule, photo album, and other personal information. Users of the system will be able to specify who can access each piece of data so that some items are private, some are only available to friends and family, and some are public. When such systems go online, businesses will be able to use the public information to pamper consumers beyond what they are currently used to. For example, if you stayed at a hotel that was using this system, the hotel could access your place in the network cloud and find out (with your permission) your favorite newspaper and tastes in music. In the morning, you might find your preferred newspaper delivered to your door along with a complimentary ticket to a concert by one of your favorite singers who happened to be in town. Once again, the amount of data and processing that such a system would require strongly suggests a P2P architecture.

I can imagine a time in the not-too-distant future where all of your devices, including home PC, cell phone, car system, and PDA, stay in constant touch with each other, storing synchronized replicas of your personal information and working with other networked computers to maintain your schedule, plan your leisure time, or even keep a daily diary of your activities. These devices could search the network to find other people who might be good friends or dating partners, and alert you when promising matches were found. In countries like Japan, teenagers are already using their cell phones for meeting others, and technology is playing an ever-increasing role in the way that they socialize (see Figure 10.7).

Smart buildings could communicate with your cell phone or PDA and adapt themselves to your preferences. For example, a room might lower its temperature when you walk in, and turn the radio to your favorite music—all courtesy of P2P computing.

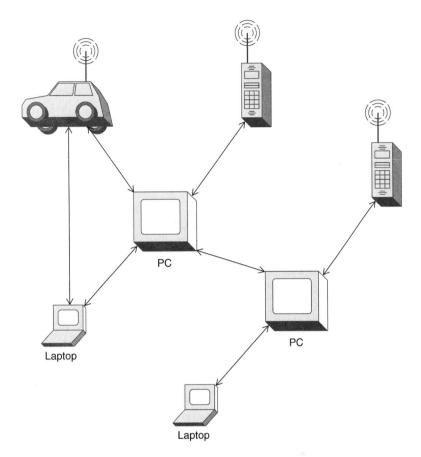

FIGURE 10.7
Everything will be linked in a P2P fashion

An even zanier idea is P2P cellular networks that use phones to perform routing as well as send and receive calls. Calls would route themselves via neighboring phones to reach their final destination. With this architecture, you could literally airdrop 10,000 cell phones into a remote region and establish an instant cellular network. I particularly like this example because the P2P architecture is clearly different from the currently established client/ server (phone/base station) approach (see Figure 10.8).

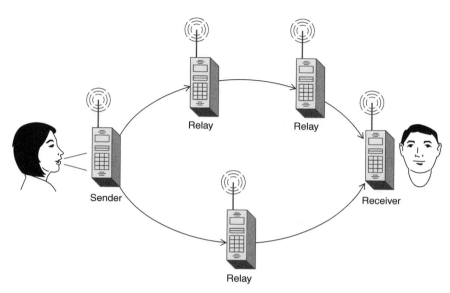

FIGURE 10.8
In a P2P phone network, phones can act as relays

Peer-To-Peer Web Services

Because web services are general purpose building blocks for creating distributed systems, they are a natural starting point for a P2P platform. WSDL exists as a means to describe a service, and UDDI allows services to be dynamically located and invoked. So what is missing?

Well, for a start, most UDDI implementations right now are centralized and not set up for publishing millions of web services. Imagine if every computer on the FastTrack network registered itself as a web service on the IBM UDDI site and every time a search occurred, a UDDI lookup occurred. The application would quickly grind to a halt. What is needed is a federated form of UDDI where information about the services as well as the search process itself is distributed among the peer nodes (see Figure 10.9).

In addition, because services can disappear with no warning in a P2P environment, support for automatic rebinding to equivalent services must be built into any P2P platform, as well as load balancing to ensure that nodes are being used wisely.

One of the biggest problems to be solved is security, especially if some web services are holding on to personal information. If data were being repli-

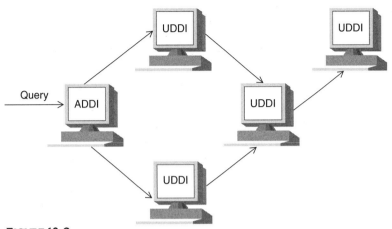

FIGURE 10.9
A federated UDDI system could work like Gnutella

cated and stored on several nodes, it would be encrypted before being distributed so that the storage nodes could not see the original data. But at some point, the data has to be retrieved and the ownership has to be verified. Representing a network identity in a way that is both decentralized and secure from hackers is a tough problem and probably the biggest hurdle for P2P systems. Microsoft is hoping that its Passport service will provide a secure identity scheme for large-scale systems, and AOL recently announced a similar service codenamed Magic Carpet. Both companies have a good track record of making life easier for consumers, so there's every reason to believe that they'll be successful and crack the problem.

One thought-provoking example of a P2P web services application is a P2P version of EBay. To use the system, you'd load an auction web service onto your home computer and tell it the things that you'd like to buy and sell. Your web service would then locate and communicate with auction web services on other computers and hunt down potential bargains, bringing good deals to your attention. Transactions would occur directly between the buyer and the seller, with no middleman to take a piece of the action. A P2P version of EBay would be more complex than a file sharing system like Napster and would benefit from the general-purpose messaging layer provided by SOAP.

An Electric Mind

There are some interesting parallels between the world of distributed computing, the development of a human brain, and the evolution of human society.

When a child is being formed in the womb, its brain cells are initially disconnected and isolated from one another. Slowly, the neurons reach out to each other with axons and dendrites, and begin to communicate with their neighbors. As the communication rate increases, neurons begin to specialize, some focused on processing sensory input, some on intermediate integration of signals, and others on high-level cognitive processing. And somehow, as a result of the interactions of a hundred billion brain cells, a mind is born (see Figure 10.10).

A similar trend toward connectedness can be found in the evolution of human society. In the early days, humans were nomads, traveling around in small tribes that rarely communicated with one another. If an invention occurred within a tribe, it was likely to die with the tribe, and even if it survived, it might take hundreds of years to propagate to other tribes. As technologies improved, tribes began to form into villages, which in turn formed into towns and cities. Mechanisms such as letters, the telegraph, and radio vastly increased the rate of communication transfer, and media like paper, film, and magnetic tape allowed human knowledge to survive beyond the generation that created it. One result of the accelerating accumulation and flow of knowledge has been an exponential growth of innovation and a rise in the collective global IQ (see Figure 10.11).

Each computer on the Internet is like a neuron in a brain or a nomad in early society. Slowly but surely, these computers are reaching out across the net-

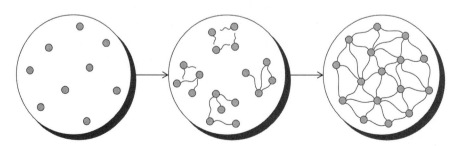

FIGURE 10.10
Neurons connect until they form a mind

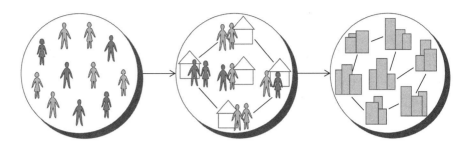

FIGURE 10.11
People connect until they form a global community

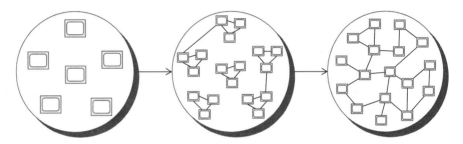

FIGURE 10.12
Do computers connect until they form an electric mind?

work and forming connections with other machines. The number of electronic messages that enter and leave a computer per year is rising every year, and P2P applications will continue to fuel this growth (see Figure 10.12).

In a fractal-like manner, there are connections within connections within connections. Each mind is formed from a web of billions of neurons. Human society is formed from a web of billions of humans. And now the Internet is forming into a new web of billions of devices. If the parallels are appropriate, there's a good chance that the Internet will evolve a mind of its own—an *electric mind*—that may prove to be mankind's greatest achievement.

Promising Insights

The biggest challenge that faces distributed computing is figuring out how to make smart, reliable systems out of dumb, unreliable parts. The fact that this can be achieved is counter-intuitive to most software developers, but there are many examples of this in nature.

For example, brain cells are continually dying and yet we do not experience a loss of continuity in our cognitive processing. In addition, research indicates than an individual neuron is a relatively low-precision device, and yet when millions of neurons operate together, they are capable of high-precision operations.

Another example is our ability to figure out the precise angle of each joint in our body even though the joint receptors are low-resolution. A joint contains a collection of receptors, each designed to send out a signal if the joint is within few degrees of a particular angle. By analyzing the output of each receptor, our brain can deduce the joint angle accurately because there's only one particular value would generate the observed distribution of outputs.

These observations suggest that there are some basic principles that operate regularly in nature than should be applicable to the creation of large-scale distributed systems.

Distributed Memory

One approach that nature adopts for storing information is to feed it into a network of processors that break it down into its constistuent components and remember it as a web of associations. The original input can be reproduced later by activating a subset of the original constituents and letting the web of associations recreate the remaining portions.

Here's a story that illustrates this approach. About 10 years ago, I was walked in a shopping mall while explaining this concept to a friend. I pointed to a sign above a shoe repair store and contrasted the way a traditional computer program would remember it versus a human brain. A traditional program would take a digital snapshot of the sign and store it on disk as an image. A brain, on the other hand, takes the image and analyzes it in a bottom-up fashion, first recognizing color blobs, lines, and curves, and then incrementally extracting higher-level features from these consistituent parts such as words, geometric relationships, and quantities of different items. The analysis and breakdown is performed by different parts of the brain, depending on the specialized behaviors of each area. For example, say the sign looked like Figure 10.13.

FIGURE 10.13
This sign can be remembered as a composite of information nuggets

A bottom-up analysis of the sign might result in the following information nuggets:

- one of the words was a man's name
- one word was above the other word
- there was a picture on the right
- there were three main visual items of interest
- there were about 10 letters
- both words ended with "s"
- one of the words begain with "j"
- one of the words contained "shoe"
- there was a picture of a shoe
- the man's name was "joe"
- the words were about the same length
- the sign was rectangular

Notice that although none of the nuggets is particularly accurate, you can deduce what the original sign probably looked like from the set of observations. Brains are remarkably good at extracting features from the environment and later recreating scenes in a detective-like way from the residuals.

There are many benefits from this approach:

1. It is highly distributed, allowing each node in the network to extract features according to its own specialization. For example, one group of nodes might be good at counting things, whereas another might specialize in geometric relationships.

2. It degrades gracefully, because as information nuggets are forgotton, the original scene can still be recreated, albeit in a less accurate form.

3. The constraint resolution process, although poorly understood, seems eminently parallelisable. Some successes in the field of neural networks, such as simulated annealing, are a small step toward understanding this mechanism.

It's particularly amusing to me that 10 years after the conversation, I still remember the information nuggets that describe the sign above the shoe store. This implies that my brain contains nuggets that remember about nuggets!

As the world moves toward decentralized information storage, insights from nature might apply to practical problems such as storing a person's profile in the network. Because a person can be described as a set of information nuggets, it should be possible to store these nuggets in various places in the network and reconstruct a profile from these nuggets when needed. The brain analogy suggests that different web services would store specific aspects of a person's profile, perhaps also having the ability to perform special processing pertaining to those aspects. For example, one set of web services could store credit information about a person and answer questions regarding the financial history, whereas another set of services could store pictures of a person and answer questions about appearance. Higher-level web services could reconstruct part or all of a person's profile by orchestrating the information nuggets held by the lower-level services.

Distributed Quality Control

Quality control is another challenge in a highly distributed environment. Take the case of the P2P education system I mentioned earlier in this chapter. If anyone is able to upload knowledge about a particular topic, how can you make sure that the knowledge is correct? One possible solution to this problem is what I call *Community Evolvable Content*. The general idea is to allow anyone in the community to add information nuggets, vote on the correctness of existing nuggets, and offer alternative, competing nuggets if they feel the current ones can be improved. Over time, the stronger nuggets would move to the foreground and the weaker nuggets would recede to the background. People could annotate a vote with the reasoning behind it, and the history of a nugget would be recorded so that anyone could examine the evolution of a particular piece of knowledge. Distributed knowledge management is a particular exciting area, ripe for innovation, and likely to be a hot topic in the years to come.

Beyond P2P

P2P is an architectural philosophy that is oriented around decentralization. To unleash the full power of P2P computing, we must learn how to build systems where data is not always synchronized, where messages are frequently lost, where nodes can vanish in moments, and where probabilities matter more than certainties.

My believe is that the computer architects of the future will be heavily influenced by the teachings of researchers like Stephen Wolfram, Douglas Hofstadter, and Marvin Minsky, who emphasize the importance of emergent behavior. Their findings indicate that to create stable large-scale systems out of small unreliable parts, you must think in terms of group dynamics rather than on an individual scale.

The next 10 years are going to be a lot of fun!

Summary

In this chapter, we saw that the trend toward decentralization is leading inexorably toward peer-to-peer architectures, and that web services are the natural foundation for P2P platforms. We also noted the parallels between the evolution of a mind, human civilization, and the Internet, and that nature may provide valuable insights for distributed computing architectures of the future.

Quiz

- Why do IT departments like three-tier architectures?
- What are the main characteristics of P2P architectures?
- What is the problem with Gnutella?
- Why is human civilization like a mind?

Exercises

1. Discuss whether neural networks are a kind of P2P network.
2. Would it be accurate to call P2P an N-tier architecture?
3. Download JXTA from Sun and experiment with some simple P2P applications.

Epilogue

I hope you find this book to be useful in your exploration of distributed computing. It's a very exciting time to be involved in this field, and there are bound to be plenty of innovations over the next few years.

My own personal efforts are focused on GAIA, the name for my company's next product. GAIA is a platform for building large-scale distributed systems that use a P2P web services architecture to achieve load balancing and fault tolerance. I'm looking forward to seeing how its P2P architecture stacks up against the more traditional architectures behind platforms like J2EE and .NET.

Feel free to send me email at graham@themindelectric.com. I welcome all feedback related to this book, as well as lively discussions on the future of distributed computing.

Sincerely,

Graham Glass

Appendix

Installing GLUE and the Examples _____

The companion CD contains two software packages:

1. GLUE, an intuitive, fast and comprehensive platform for web services.

2. The source code and .jar file for all the examples in the book.

The software may be installed and run on any computer that supports the Java Developer Kit (JDK) 1.1 or above. You can download the latest version of the JDK from http://java.sun.com/j2se/.

The top-level contents of the CD are laid out as follows:

```
electric // top level directory for GLUE, readme.html
  bin // command line tools: wsdl2java, java2wsdl and console
  docs // root of all documentation (HTML and PDF)
  lib // GLUE-STD.jar, GLUE-EXAMPLES.jar and standard extension .jars
  src // root of GLUE source code and GLUE examples
  webapps // web application for console
```

```
wsbook // top level directory for all examples in this book
   lib // WSBOOK.jar, the .jar of all examples in this book
   src // root of source code for all examples in this book
```

To minimize the installation process, copy the contents of the CD into the root directory of your hard drive, thereby creating top-level directories in your hard drive called \electric and \wsbook. Then perform the following steps:

- Add \electric\lib\GLUE-STD.jar and \wsbook\lib\WSBOOK.jar to your CLASSPATH as well as the standard Java extension libraries servlet.jar and jnet.jar. The \electric\lib directory includes these standard extensions for your convenience.
- If you want to use HTTPS for secure web services, add the standard Java extension libraries jsse.jar and jcert.jar to your CLASSPATH.
- If you want to use the console, set your operating system's environment variable ELECTRIC_HOME to the top-level GLUE directory. For example, if you copied the CD contents to the root directory of your hard drive, you'd set ELECTRIC_HOME to "\electric".
- Finally, to use the GLUE command line tools, add \electric\bin to your command path setting. On Windows, this involves updating your PATH environment variable.

You are now ready to use GLUE and execute the examples in the book.

Here are some useful links:

- GLUE documentation: /electric/readme.html
- GLUE support: http://groups.yahoo.com/group/MindElectricTechnology
- GLUE home page: http://www.themindelectric.com/products/glue/glue.html

Resources

SOAP

SOAP specification: http://www.w3.org/TR/SOAP/

WSDL specification: http://www.w3.org/TR/wsdl

UDDI

Main site: http://www.uddi.org/

Data structure reference: http://www.uddi.org/pubs/UDDI_XML_Structure_Reference.pdf

API reference: http://www.uddi.org/pubs/UDDI_Programmers_API_Specification.pdf

Technical White Paper: http://www.uddi.org/pubs/Iru_UDDI_Technical_White_Paper.pdf

Executive White Paper: http://www.uddi.org/pubs/UDDI_Executive_White_Paper.pdf

UDDI4J: http://oss.software.ibm.com/developerworks/projects/uddi4j

IBM UDDI registry: https://www-3.ibm.com/services/uddi/protect/registry.html

Microsoft UDDI registry: http://uddi.microsoft.com

GLUE UDDI: http://www.themindelectric.com/products/uddi/uddi.html

General Web Service Sites

Web services resource center: http://www.soap-wrc.com/webservices/default.asp

Vendor-neutral web services portal: http://www.webservices.org/

XMethods web services portal: http://www.xmethods.net

Companies/Products

Microsoft/.NET: http://www.microsoft.com/net/default.asp

IBM/WebSphere: http://www.ibm.com

IBM/Web Services Toolkit: http://www.alphaworks.ibm.com/tech/webservices-toolkit

BEA/WebLogic: http://www.bea.com

The Mind Electric/GLUE: http://www.themindelectric.com

Apache SOAP: http://xml.apache.org/soap/index.html

Idoox/WASP: http://www.idoox.com

CapeClear: http://www.capeclear.com

SilverStream/JBroker: http://www.silverstream.com

Iona/XMLBus: http://www.iona.com

SOAP::Lite: http://www.soaplite.com

P2P

MojoNation: http://www.mojonation.com

Napster: http://www.napster.com

Gnutella: http://gnutella.wego.com

FastTrack: http://www.fasttrack.nu

JXTA: http://www.jxta.org

XML

Main site: http://www.w3.org/XML/W3C
XML specification: http://www.w3.org/TR/REC-xml
Namespaces specification: http://www.w3.org/TR/REC-xml-names/
XPath specification: http://www.w3.org/TR/xpath
XML Schema for Datatypes: http://www.w3.org/TR/xmlschema-2/
Electric XML: http://www.themindelectric.com/products/xml/xml.html
JDOM: http://www.jdom.org
DOM4J: http://www.dom4j.org

Miscellaneous

Blake's seven fan site: http://www.btinternet.com/~blakes.seven/

Index

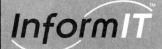

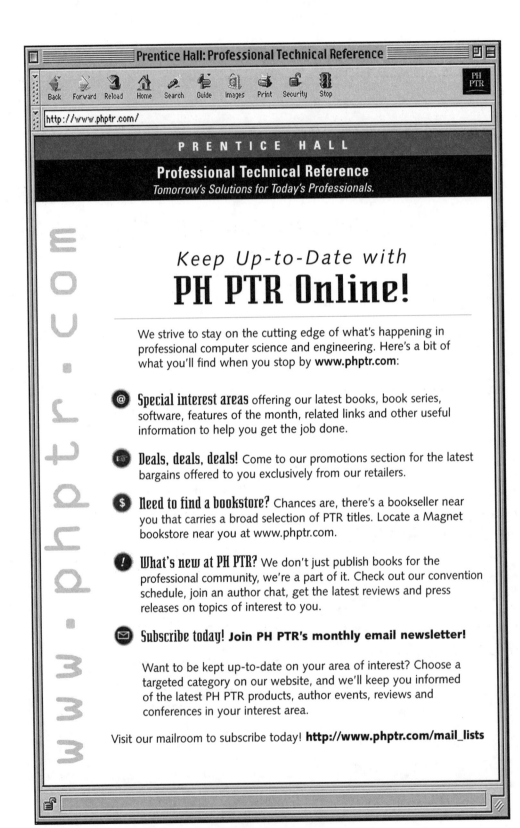

LICENSE AGREEMENT AND LIMITED WARRANTY

READ THE FOLLOWING TERMS AND CONDITIONS CAREFULLY BEFORE OPENING THIS SOFTWARE MEDIA PACKAGE. THIS LEGAL DOCUMENT IS AN AGREEMENT BETWEEN YOU AND PRENTICE-HALL, INC. (THE "COMPANY"). BY OPENING THIS SEALED SOFTWARE MEDIA PACKAGE, YOU ARE AGREEING TO BE BOUND BY THESE TERMS AND CONDITIONS. IF YOU DO NOT AGREE WITH THESE TERMS AND CONDITIONS, DO NOT OPEN THE SOFTWARE MEDIA PACKAGE. PROMPTLY RETURN THE UNOPENED SOFTWARE MEDIA PACKAGE AND ALL ACCOMPANYING ITEMS TO THE PLACE YOU OBTAINED THEM FOR A FULL REFUND OF ANY SUMS YOU HAVE PAID.

1. **GRANT OF LICENSE:** In consideration of your payment of the license fee, which is part of the price you paid for this product, and your agreement to abide by the terms and conditions of this Agreement, the Company grants to you a nonexclusive right to use and display the copy of the enclosed software program (hereinafter the "SOFTWARE") on a single computer (i.e., with a single CPU) at a single location so long as you comply with the terms of this Agreement. The Company reserves all rights not expressly granted to you under this Agreement.

2. **OWNERSHIP OF SOFTWARE:** You own only the magnetic or physical media (the enclosed SOFTWARE) on which the SOFTWARE is recorded or fixed, but the Company retains all the rights, title, and ownership to the SOFTWARE recorded on the original SOFTWARE copy(ies) and all subsequent copies of the SOFTWARE, regardless of the form or media on which the original or other copies may exist. This license is not a sale of the original SOFTWARE or any copy to you.

3. **COPY RESTRICTIONS:** This SOFTWARE and the accompanying printed materials and user manual (the "Documentation") are the subject of copyright. You may not copy the Documentation or the SOFTWARE, except that you may make a single copy of the SOFTWARE for backup or archival purposes only. You may be held legally responsible for any copying or copyright infringement which is caused or encouraged by your failure to abide by the terms of this restriction.

4. **USE RESTRICTIONS:** You may not network the SOFTWARE or otherwise use it on more than one computer or computer terminal at the same time. You may physically transfer the SOFTWARE from one computer to another provided that the SOFTWARE is used on only one computer at a time. You may not distribute copies of the SOFTWARE or Documentation to others. You may not reverse engineer, disassemble, decompile, modify, adapt, translate, or create derivative works based on the SOFTWARE or the Documentation without the prior written consent of the Company.

5. **TRANSFER RESTRICTIONS:** The enclosed SOFTWARE is licensed only to you and may not be transferred to any one else without the prior written consent of the Company. Any unauthorized transfer of the SOFTWARE shall result in the immediate termination of this Agreement.

6. **TERMINATION:** This license is effective until terminated. This license will terminate automatically without notice from the Company and become null and void if you fail to comply with any provisions or limitations of this license. Upon termination, you shall destroy the Documentation and all copies of the SOFTWARE. All provisions of this Agreement as to warranties, limitation of liability, remedies or damages, and our ownership rights shall survive termination.

7. **MISCELLANEOUS:** This Agreement shall be construed in accordance with the laws of the United States of America and the State of New York and shall benefit the Company, its affiliates, and assignees.

8. **LIMITED WARRANTY AND DISCLAIMER OF WARRANTY:** The Company warrants that the SOFTWARE, when properly used in accordance with the Documentation, will operate in substantial conformity with the description of the SOFTWARE set forth in the Documentation. The Company does not warrant that the SOFTWARE will meet your requirements or that the operation of the SOFTWARE will be uninterrupted or error-free. The Company warrants that the

media on which the SOFTWARE is delivered shall be free from defects in materials and workmanship under normal use for a period of thirty (30) days from the date of your purchase. Your only remedy and the Company's only obligation under these limited warranties is, at the Company's option, return of the warranted item for a refund of any amounts paid by you or replacement of the item. Any replacement of SOFTWARE or media under the warranties shall not extend the original warranty period. The limited warranty set forth above shall not apply to any SOFTWARE which the Company determines in good faith has been subject to misuse, neglect, improper installation, repair, alteration, or damage by you. EXCEPT FOR THE EXPRESSED WARRANTIES SET FORTH ABOVE, THE COMPANY DISCLAIMS ALL WARRANTIES, EXPRESS OR IMPLIED, INCLUDING WITHOUT LIMITATION, THE IMPLIED WARRANTIES OF MERCHANTABILITY AND FITNESS FOR A PARTICULAR PURPOSE. EXCEPT FOR THE EXPRESS WARRANTY SET FORTH ABOVE, THE COMPANY DOES NOT WARRANT, GUARANTEE, OR MAKE ANY REPRESENTATION REGARDING THE USE OR THE RESULTS OF THE USE OF THE SOFTWARE IN TERMS OF ITS CORRECTNESS, ACCURACY, RELIABILITY, CURRENTNESS, OR OTHERWISE.

IN NO EVENT, SHALL THE COMPANY OR ITS EMPLOYEES, AGENTS, SUPPLIERS, OR CONTRACTORS BE LIABLE FOR ANY INCIDENTAL, INDIRECT, SPECIAL, OR CONSEQUENTIAL DAMAGES ARISING OUT OF OR IN CONNECTION WITH THE LICENSE GRANTED UNDER THIS AGREEMENT, OR FOR LOSS OF USE, LOSS OF DATA, LOSS OF INCOME OR PROFIT, OR OTHER LOSSES, SUSTAINED AS A RESULT OF INJURY TO ANY PERSON, OR LOSS OF OR DAMAGE TO PROPERTY, OR CLAIMS OF THIRD PARTIES, EVEN IF THE COMPANY OR AN AUTHORIZED REPRESENTATIVE OF THE COMPANY HAS BEEN ADVISED OF THE POSSIBILITY OF SUCH DAMAGES. IN NO EVENT SHALL LIABILITY OF THE COMPANY FOR DAMAGES WITH RESPECT TO THE SOFTWARE EXCEED THE AMOUNTS ACTUALLY PAID BY YOU, IF ANY, FOR THE SOFTWARE.

SOME JURISDICTIONS DO NOT ALLOW THE LIMITATION OF IMPLIED WARRANTIES OR LIABILITY FOR INCIDENTAL, INDIRECT, SPECIAL, OR CONSEQUENTIAL DAMAGES, SO THE ABOVE LIMITATIONS MAY NOT ALWAYS APPLY. THE WARRANTIES IN THIS AGREEMENT GIVE YOU SPECIFIC LEGAL RIGHTS AND YOU MAY ALSO HAVE OTHER RIGHTS WHICH VARY IN ACCORDANCE WITH LOCAL LAW.

ACKNOWLEDGMENT

YOU ACKNOWLEDGE THAT YOU HAVE READ THIS AGREEMENT, UNDERSTAND IT, AND AGREE TO BE BOUND BY ITS TERMS AND CONDITIONS. YOU ALSO AGREE THAT THIS AGREEMENT IS THE COMPLETE AND EXCLUSIVE STATEMENT OF THE AGREEMENT BETWEEN YOU AND THE COMPANY AND SUPERSEDES ALL PROPOSALS OR PRIOR AGREEMENTS, ORAL, OR WRITTEN, AND ANY OTHER COMMUNICATIONS BETWEEN YOU AND THE COMPANY OR ANY REPRESENTATIVE OF THE COMPANY RELATING TO THE SUBJECT MATTER OF THIS AGREEMENT.

Should you have any questions concerning this Agreement or if you wish to contact the Company for any reason, please contact in writing at the address below.

Robin Short
Prentice Hall PTR
One Lake Street
Upper Saddle River, New Jersey 07458